Nourish Inspirations

Shamika King

Nourish Inspirations

Copyright © 2019 by Shamika King.

Self-published, edited, and formatted by Shamika King.

All Scripture quotations are used from the Holy Bible.

ISBN No. 9781695398306

Acknowledgement

All Glory to God! Who placed me here to be a living example and a servant of Jesus Christ. All Glory to God! who placed me here to serve you Nourish Inspirations and Words of Encouragement, so that you may choose to seek him first, repent, turn away from sin, be saved, redeemed, and healed for eternity. For every word of wisdom written, did not come from me but from God through Jesus Christ, through the Holy Spirit, through me. Should you feel inspired and uplifted by these words of wisdom, please boast about our heavenly father who dwells in heaven because it all comes from him.

All Glory to God forever and ever! Amen.

-Galatians 1:5NLT

Be a good steward over what you have. Don't worry about or rush to get what you don't have. Be grateful, content, and humble yourself.

Gone

Remember all those times you would say "noooo no, put that back, that's mines" However, before the day would end, you'd change your mind and say, "go head and take it, that's fine." I wish I can hear your voice, if I ever had to choose bringing you back would be my first choice.

Bored, always trying to find something to do, every now and then it drives me insane just knowing I can no longer call on your name. Out of nowhere here comes the shedding of my tears, it happens every time I try to picture myself living without you for the remaining of my years. I still have your number stored in my phone, it helps me imagine that you're here, Lord please forgive me, but I refuse to accept the fact that my grandma is gone.

At times like this I would call and say "Ma, what is it that you need me to do for you?" I always came running on my two feet, no wonder you nicknamed me too-sweet, if no one else did...I would, and you knew. You might've been a headache to others, but you were never a burden to me, with you it was impossible for me to be through.

Although I try to smile and play it nice, I'm learning that God's grace, strength, and mercy is the only way I can survive through this beautiful, yet unfair thing called life. Too much to gain, so I take my time as I slowly digest this never-ending pain.

I understood the meaning behind "there's a time and a place for everything" until that time and place came when God called you home my whole comprehension of that meaning changed. Lost, so I panicked. Never been diagnosed but I could've sworn I was schizophrenic. I questioned God "why her? when I know for a fact you could've taken anything." People talk about hurt, yet this here was a different kind of hurt that lingered far beyond just a sting.

Late nights, early morning, I be up crying, tossing and turning. I know God make no mistakes, but this just don't feel right... it's all wrong, Lord please forgive me, but I refuse to accept the fact that my grandma is Gone.

Poetry By: Shamika King

Understanding is not only a comprehension of what's being communicated. It's a level of respect for what may not always be agreed on.

Failure

*Try not to be humiliated and/or alarmed when you fail. Based off your expectations, I know it may not look or feel good to you or others but believe it or not, failure is apart of success. **For example**: When you fail at something and learn from it, what happens? You succeed and proceed to the next level, right? And when you succeed in life you become grateful and thank God for all those times you failed, right? Of course, you do. Why because if you hadn't failed, you wouldn't have come to that place of success.*

Most of us would rather jump right to the top. I mean if you think about it, it's easier that way. Who wouldn't want to take the effortless route out? The unchallenging way will always get you there rapidly, however, it'll be the very reason why you hit rock bottom even faster than you got to the top. Why? Simply because no pressure was presented for you to learn. Due to no pressure being presented, no knowledge was gained. If there is no knowledge gained, how can you succeed and what can you possibly use to win again?

Most of us would rather not deal with any kind of pressure, disappointments, criticism, distractions, temptations, or mistakes. We most certainly don't want to deal with being alone during the process. So, what most of us do is we spend more time procrastinating about all the possibilities of failing. Also, we allow the limits in which we place on ourselves, to hold us back.

For example: Most of us will start something, such as; a job, a business, a learning course, a friendship and/or a relationship. Everything will start off going very well until at some point more is expected of us. It can be more time, more compassion, more hard work, being more transparent, or setting boundaries. When situations like this come about, most of us begin to fear the unknown, procrastinate, and overthink everything. From there on, we run from the pressure that only presented itself for us to grow and overcome many obstacles. Not only do we run from it, we become frustrated, bypass, and place many opportunities on hold; believing that we're incapable of being successful.

If you can't gain self- control, have patience, endure hardships, mature, be open-minded, and become stable, not perfect but stable enough to remain faithful to handle any kind of pressure, disappointments, criticism, distractions, temptations, mistakes, and alone time to focus and build, then there's a possibility that you wouldn't be able to handle being successful. The reason I say this is because all these substantial, yet devastating essentials is a necessity for you to succeed.

Failure was never designed for us to fail, it was choreographed for us to succeed. However, when we become disconcert and aghast, we misinterpret the real definition regarding failure. We then, begin to devalue ourselves by solely believing that we're not proficient of being Prosperous.

Try not to be blinded by the mistake, to the point where you've missed the message.

Storm

I could go on and on about the many ways it came, sometimes it hit me back to back, other times it occurred unexpectedly, however, each experience was never the same.

When it rained, it poured, after so many attempts of trying, I gave up in the midst and decided to surrender all to the Lord. Day and night, I felt like I couldn't get out of the dark, everything seem like it would never be alright. Times like this reminds me of John 8:12, when Jesus said he is the light.

I questioned God, "how long would this last? Take it away! does this have anything to do with my past?" I was all alone as I kept trying to explain, looking at my outer appearance, people would say, "Yeah right, you ain't in no pain."

I got too comfortable, yet it only came temporarily to shape and strip me. Too busy overthinking and complaining, so I disguised the meaning of it, concluding that it was the reason why I was unable to see. There I was again, stuck never realizing the lesson on being the best it knew I could be.

Now I understand the true meaning behind every time it arrives, it taught me to have faith, blossom, and sprout as I continue to move forward and strive.

If you can fix it, then fix it. If not… learn from it, grow from it, and keep moving forward.

Hey You

Hey, You… Why are you always sad, walking with you head down? You mean to tell me, that there's nothing great about life that can motivate you to wipe away that frown.

Are you aware that you're a Queen? Are you aware that you're a King? Sitting around wasting time, what's really on your mind? why you playing? You've been built with so much potential, believe it or not, you're a necessity, you're very substantial. Don't look at me crazy, I'm just saying.

Hey, You… Why do you allow other people to get the best of you? You always yelling, "I give up! You made me this way! I'm through!" Chile, people will be people, they'll never understand your life sequel. So, go ahead and learn from the pressure; besides, it'll only be for a little while.

Why are you afraid to look in the mirror? Oh, I understand. When you see yourself, you see how you feel, you're view is deep in the interior. That's the stress that comes with growth as you progress, however, you'll forever be capable to stand.

Hey, You… I know you love hard, you have a big heart. But why do you give it all away at once? Why not slowly let down your guard? Hurt people will manipulate you just to take charge, you got to be more careful Love, or they'll tare you apart.

Poetry By: Shamika King

Don't allow the storm to stop you from shining.

Father God

You're so miraculous to me, All I desire to do is apply, abide, and spread your word. You knew that your purpose for me wouldn't be easy, seeing that many people vision can sometimes be blurred.

Your love and compassion are beyond my understanding. As I do your Will, you never expect me to be perfect. Therefore, I never hesitate to get before you completely naked.

Do you remember that dream I had back in 2016? I'll never forget walking with you and listening as you told me to live righteous and remain faithful. Since then, I've remained in your presence as I continuously seek and build a never-ending relationship with you. Thank You, Father God, I'm grateful.

You deserve all the glory, if it wasn't for you, I would've never survived to share my painful, yet inspirational story. What you planned for me, no man can stop. No matter how many times I fall, with you by my side, I will forever stand tall and exceed to the top.

Every time I worry, I run and isolate myself until I think about your word in 1 Peter 5:7, it says, "Give all your worries and cares to God, for he cares about you". I, then, snap back to reality and walk by faith, knowing that you will pull me through.

Your Word, Psalms 63:6 says, "I lie awake thinking of you, meditating on you through the night". In those times, when

I cry and procrastinate, you always comfort me. You're always so serene when you whisper, "Everything is going to be alright, just trust me".

When I'm sick spiritually, mentally, and emotionally; you're my medicine. For years, I turned to others for help and healing, until I surrendered all to you. I learned that when it comes to you, there's simply no comparison. Father God, you're all I need. Yes, you're enough and I'm so glad that you called and chose me to be your living seed.

Poetry By: Shamika King

Some people change and some never do. Either way, you shouldn't allow someone else decision to hinder you from what you decide is best for you.

Love

Oh! How I Love, Love. Everything about it springs naturally from the one who lives not only within me but secures me from above.

Seldomly does it fail, no matter what I do or how far I run, it remains faithful, surpassing my knowledge, yet I'm grateful. Whoever said it hurts must've been confused after that strong dose of lust, mistaken for Love, in which left them abused.

Oh! How I Love, Love. It captivated me without force, guiding me down the right path, doing what it takes to prevent me from going blind. So gentle and peculiar, no one believes me when I express the way it comforts me; Would you? If I shared how it goes beyond measures leaving me speechless, while blowing my mind?

Installed within me, I couldn't resist the way it sprouted from my heart, it was eccentric leaving me indecisive trying to cope with the fact that nothing can separate or tare it a part.

Oh! How I Love, Love. I didn't choose Love. Love chose me, yet I couldn't repel it, so I had to choose Love. Created right along with me before the foundation of earth, resided in everything about me since before the day my mother gave birth.

I tried so many times, but I couldn't fake it, it was like running away from the wind, impossible for me to escape it. With or without my perspective, believe it or not, it will forever be effective.

Oh! How I Love, Love. Catalyzed by God; the definition of Love, no longer do I wonder about the many reasons I am drawn to Love. As I live on, I understand to be loved is to Love.

Poetry By: Shamika King

A tough stumble is required in every trial.

Going Through

A couple of days ago after spending one on one time with God and mediating on his Word, I learned that there are two different ways of Going Through. You can go through in Peace or you can go through in Distress. What do I mean by that?

When a difficult trial come to test you, instead of panicking, you remain humble. Instead of rushing the process, you remain patient as you walk by faith and not by sight. Instead of coming to your own understanding and trying to handle the situation, you lean strictly towards God and go based off his understanding.

Trust in the Lord with all your heart; do not depend on your own understanding. -Proverbs 3:5NLT

It's not always about what happens to you that matters, however, it's about how you react to what happens to you. So, if you react out of Peace to the difficult trial in which you're going through, then, you will go through in Peace. It doesn't matter if your end results are good or bad, you will be at peace. You will also gain knowledge from the difficult trial. This will strengthen your Faith and motivate you to not panic, run, and complain during tough times. As you go about many situations that approach you like this, your faith alone will rapidly catch the attention of God. He will than show you his favor and grant you more of his Peace to face the battle.

May the Lord show you his favor and give you his peace.

-Numbers 6:26

Now when a difficult trial come to test you, if you should choose Fear, which is the opposite of Faith, in most cases, you will find yourself constantly feeling drained and hindered by things and people. You will find yourself worrying while always trying to control and make a way, based off what you think is best. This does nothing but trigger the distractions and temptations around and within you even more. Before you know it, you'll find yourself complaining about the same things repeatedly while questioning God "why you?"

This causes you to miss the lesson from the test that came through the difficult trial. This also causes you to stay hindered and blinded in a season with things and people that you were suppose to be delivered from years ago. When you react out of Fear, you begin to doubt yourself and question your character, joy, peace, and faith. Reacting out of Fear also hinders you from learning and it prolongs your destiny.

The Lord himself will fight for you, just stay calm. -Exodus 14:14

I know at times you may find yourself battling with both, however, in most cases Fear outweighs Faith. Although your Faith should outweigh your Fear, it's rare. Why? Because most of us have been overly independent that we have no time to sit around and wait, let alone trust God. This explains why most of us only know one way of going through and that would be Going through in Distress.

    If you've been Going through the same things for extended periods of time just to end up back at square one, chances are you've been walking in Fear. Take some time to examine yourself and please be honest with yourself. Just think about all the times something difficult hit you unexpectedly, what was your reaction? I just want you to try to understand that when you are going through tough times, you are not alone, so try not to be afraid to face it. I believe that some where down the line you will choose peace.

When you go through rivers of difficulty, you will not drown. When you walk through the fire of oppression, you will not be burned up; the flames will not consume you. -Isaiah 43:2NLT

What happened to you might've caught you by surprise, however, it wasn't a surprise to God. God can use any hardship for his Glory.

Afraid

Here we go again, I was so close that nothing could convince me to stop. Headed to the top, my mind captivated me… hindering me, to the point where I deceived myself believing that I could never win.

I was so brave and courageous, yet the way my mind lingered, I was afraid it would overtake me. I had to step away from people at times because I didn't want it to spread. I'm trying to heal, not kill and so I had to be careful not to get carried away in my head, this thing here was outrageous. I know my heart is pure, yes, I'm always so sincere but most people truly had no idea.

At times I wandered off into this dark place, almost similar to a cave, I would cry out to God saying "Lord I if I die, please come and get me. Don't let these demons I struggle with habituate my soul. I love living for you but sometimes this life can be so cold."

One minute I'm up on the go, the next my faith is wavering, and I find myself discouraged, just going with the flow. I know I was born with a purpose, no wonder my spirit refuse to prolong and settle with me saying no, It's just that at times I can get so nervous.

I know I'm not the only one who have to endure and run this race, I always seem to stand, it never hurt to keep a smile on my face. People ask me how I do it, I inspire them to keep believing and trust God's Grace.

Yet and still they get mad, they secretly hate me and every chance they get, they try to beat me down. Late in the night, I lay in my bed and wonder should I keep moving or isolate myself and not utter a sound.

This one here was definitely a tough fight, the only way to escape was for me to walk by faith and not by sight. A lot of times I just want to give up and be through, but then I wonder, what will I do? In times like this I think of God's Word, Psalms 56:3, it says; But when I am afraid, I will put my trust in you.

Poetry By: Shamika King

Faith and Feelings doesn't mix. So, if you ever plan on walking by Faith, get out of your feelings.

Surrender

More than rare I hear a lot of people say, "I would never take that to God. I can handle that myself. I just need God to handle this for me and I'll be alright". What I've realized overtime is that the things we as people think we have under control, we really don't. Because we don't have what we think we have under control, one thing leads to another. We then, pick and choose what we need Gods help with.

For example*: I myself, use to pick and choose. I treated God like the people around me. I didn't really trust him, so I told him what I wanted him to know. I only went to him when I wanted something or when I needed help in what I felt I needed help in. Most times, I only brought the icing to God, not the cake because to be honest with you, I wasn't ready to face myself and surrender all to him.*

During this time in my life, I was either moving but still stuck or I kept finding myself repeating dysfunctional behaviors and cycles. I couldn't figure out for the life of me why I was hindered and unable to grow. I had gotten to a place in my life where I was completely fed up with myself. This is when I decided to stop giving God bits and pieces of me and chose to surrender all of me.

Now, of course, I know I'm not the only one who has experienced this. There are others who are currently experiencing this or may have surpass this. I just want to encourage you on this day to surrender it all to God. Whatever it is you're going through within and/or around you, surrender it all to God. God is aware of what you're going through and how much it bothers you. He would love to help but he will never force his way in on you. He grants us all free will to open completely and surrender all to him.

If you think you have it all under control, you're only deceiving yourself. Trust me, I once use to think that myself. If you want to be redeemed from it all and produce the fruits of the spirit, you should get down to the root of the cause, be willing to repent, and surrender it all. You have to face yourself and understand that you're only human and it's only so much that you can bear. I know at times it can be difficult to trust and surrender to God. I know that you've become comfortable with depression, stress, and pain to the point where redemption scares you and make you feel uncomfortable.

From experience, I've learned that those things that made me feel uncomfortable was the best thing that ever happen to me. It helped me become the woman and mother that I am today. Many of us have become selfish, not just with others but with ourselves. Because we're selfish with ourselves, most of us feel that we must be overly independent and strong during times we should be transparent, submissive, and humble.

This overwhelms us and because we don't want to face the root of the issue, we throw God bits and pieces, hoping that he would make us feel even more comfortable. The God I serve always makes sure I'm uncomfortable, ready, and prepared. He desires for me to be free, filled, and produce the fruits of the spirit. However, I had to be willing to trust him wholeheartedly and surrender all to him.

Surrender all to God and slowly but surely watch your life and everything about you change for the better. This won't be easy, but it will most certainly be worth it. This won't make you feel comfortable, however rejoice and be glad for every uncomfortable moment that you experience. It will give your faith a chance to grow and strengthen you to overcome many obstacles.

The best choice you could ever make in life, is to give up Control and choose Peace.

You're Still Worthy

You're a good man, you're a good woman. Yes, you're still worthy.

You may not be perfect but you're stable, you may not be perfect but you're faithful. Trust me when I say you're able - you're still worthy

Don't let nobody knock you off your square, yeah so what you may sweat every now and then, let 'em stare - you're still worthy

Tired of crying, too much to bear, sick of people tryna play you like a fool, steady treating you unfair. Fed up with all the lying, blinded by the fact that they keep taking advantage of you, the more you play it cool, regardless though -you're still worthy

Always in need of a shoulder but who can you really trust to lean on? it's hard, I know...so you just gotta move on. Everybody walking around bleeding bad on the inside, yet their actions got you acting like you bolder, like you really ain't in need of another shoulder -you're still worthy

No matter what, guard your heart and remain humble, to be honest you got to in order to learn and grow. You gotta understand that real trials require a tough stumble -you're still worthy

Why do you let these people get the best of you? Now you walking around with your head down. Deep in your thoughts, ain't got time for nothing, not even you. You don't wanna hear it, even if they got you looking like a clown, yet you steady yelling "I just wanna be through" Here comes the one that's truly meant for you, now what you gone do? Make 'em struggle to see and bring out the best in you? -you're still worthy

Don't know if you're going or coming. You want out but you been feeling trapped in, is it that you scared to end just to begin? I'm not saying it's easy, just go for it and watch yourself win   -you're still worthy

No rest, low self-esteem, lack of confidence, and depressed. Why do you let people treat you like you're on parole? You must've forgot how powerful you are. You must've forgot you've already been equipped with everything you need to be in control -you're still worthy

Never let 'em beat you down and captivate your inner joy. You're here for a reason, so get up, forgive, let go, and be free. Don't allow that person, thing, or even yourself, hinder your abilities and treat you like a worthless toy - you're still worthy

Poetry By: Shamika King

The change you desire to see, must first begin within you.

We Need You

More than rare, I see a lot of people depressed, drained, feeling like a mistake, lost, having suicidal thoughts, behaving selfish, and just about ready to give up, if they haven't already given up. This hasn't only been people around me, but it has been me and I'm sure it's probably been you. We've all been on the edge, convincing ourselves to jump. Convincing ourselves to believe every negative thing about ourselves, as if our existence doesn't serve a purpose.

However, somehow, we still seem to manage and so we keep moving. We're beat down but we keep moving. We may feel like a mistake, but we keep moving. We may want to give up so bad, but we keep moving. Most of us may have suicidal thoughts but we don't take our lives, instead we keep moving. Do you know why you keep moving? Do you know why once you give up one day, you get back up the next day? Why? Because deep within you know that there's still hope in this wicked world that continuously try to captivate you and make you feel like you'll never be capable to rise and cope.

Why? Because before the foundation of earth, you were created to fulfill Gods Purpose. Why? Because you may be feeling many different ways about yourself, people and things but your spirit is always ready to fulfill Gods Will. Why? Because there's something within you that's needed. Yes, that's right! There's something within you that's needed.

I need you, he needs you, she needs you, we need you, they need you. That's why you just keep moving. You might've stop believing in you, but God still believes in you. You might've given up on yourself, but God hasn't given up on you. Why? Because I need you, he needs you, she needs you, we need you, they need you. Now I know everything is not for everybody but there's something in everybody for somebody.

For Example:

You tired of singing, but that song was poured in you to produce freely, so people can listen and be healed. You tired of writing, but those books were created within you to redeem millions of people. You tired of speaking but you were born with a voice so powerful to encourage and motivate thousands of people. You tired of drawing, but your art was designed within you to produce for people. It was designed so they can experience peace, joy, and freedom from the moment they lay their eyes on it. You may be tired but don't give up, keep moving. Why? Because I need you, he needs you, she needs you, we need you, they need you.

Everything you're doing matters, especially when it's coming pure from the heart. There's someone out there that need to hear your testimony. They desire to know, when did it start, how did you overcome it, who inspired you, and brought you out. There's someone out there that's going through the same thing you're going through and they need what you have within you to produce, so that they can truly know that there's hope and be set free.

Don't give up! Keep moving and hear me when I say you are not alone. I know it may seem or feel like It, but you are not alone. You matter, you are a masterpiece, you are loved, you are important, you're still worthy, you're way too valuable and you are needed. Please don't stop now! Do it for me, do it for her, do it for him. Do it for them, do it for us. A lot of times we stop and give up because we grow selfish, thinking that everything we produce is for ourselves. When we grow selfish, we blocked our ability to overcome, learn and grow from the trials in our life. When this happens, we start thinking selfishly and we can't properly produce what's been placed within us to set others free.

We start feeling like we don't matter, and we're not needed, so we hate, compete, and take from others just to end up with nothing, not knowing we ourselves have plenty of fruit to produce and give. Once more, I just want you to know that you matter, you are a masterpiece, you are loved, you are important, you're still worthy, you're way too valuable and you are needed. So please don't be discourage, don't give up and keep moving. We Need You.

No matter what may occur, choose to Love Yourself.

Get out of the way

Overtime, I realized that God wants me to live my life. The best gift he's given all of us is Free Will. Free Will is not to be taken advantage of, nor is it to draw us far away from God. It's for us to learn, grow, and use every opportunity to draw closer to God. It's for us to freely choose to be a willing vessel, not a perfect vessel.

If you want what's best for another individual like you say you do, show it with your actions and get out the way. If you want what's best for you, walk by faith, not by sight and get out of the way. I say this because more than rare, you can get in your own way, not the devil or anyone else...but you.

*A lot of times, we get in the way and don't even realize it. We strongly desire another individual to get it together. We threaten them to get it together and force them to understand our outlook on their life. More than rare, it's only for our selfish reasons. **For example:** You may want your man/woman, husband, wife, children, friends, or family member to get it together so that they can make you feel whole and/or complete about yourself. You don't fully want them to do it for the sake of themselves but only because it would be beneficial to you or make you feel in control.*

If you truly love and care for them, you would get out the way. You would let them get many different doses of life. You would let them hit rock bottom, watch them climb to the top, watch them learn, grow, and prosper. You will witness how they transformed from reckless, careless, and selfish…into a compassionate, wisdom-filled, loving individual. However, you have to get out the way so that they can find their way.

*The more you stay in the way, chances are they will continue to be confused, lost, spoiled, irresponsible, and they will blame you for everything, to make themselves feel justified. **For example:** Imagine being on a crowded bus. Everybody is in everybody way. Now when someone shows a sign that it's time for them to get off, you have to get out the way or you might just have to step off the bus yourself, to get completely out of their way. Now imagine if you don't get out way, things begin to get hectic. They lose control and whether you want to admit it or not, it drives you insane.*

Not only that but they will end up with you in a place they have no business at. It may be a good place but because they didn't experience that space to walk their own path without anyone in the way, they will take advantage of it. I say all this to simply say once more…Get out of the way if you want those who are dear to your heart to find the right way.

An inheritance obtained too early in life is not a blessing in the end.
- Proverbs 20:21NLT

If there's an entrance, there's an exit. You may not leave out the same way you entered, but there's always a way out. The question is, do you want to get out?

I'm Not Perfect

Remember it is sin to know what you ought to do and then not do it. -James 4:17NLT

Maybe it's you, someone you know, or maybe you've witness numerous people yelling "I'm Not Perfect" To be completely honest it used to be me. I didn't want to hear the truth, why? Because the truth reveals and redeems. I was so use to bondage that I had no intentions on being redeemed. I had so many selfish ways and skeletons in my closet, that I was ashamed of and most certainly wasn't ready to be revealed.

Even during those times where I did as I pleased, I knew what was right from wrong. However, I just wasn't ready to accept what I knew. I wasn't ready to understand what I knew. Anytime someone tried to correct me with the powerful truth regarding my wrongdoings, I felt like they were being judge-mental. Most times I would lose control and yell at them trying to get them to understand that I wasn't perfect.

Truth of the matter is, I had judging and the truth mixed up. I allowed myself to get comfortable with my imperfections that I used them to the core and made myself feel justified. I used my imperfections as an excuse to continuously do wrong.

What I've come to learn overtime, is that no one is perfect, however, just because you're not perfect doesn't mean you can't do right. Just because you're not perfect doesn't mean you have to continuously make yourself feel justified. Just because you're not perfect, doesn't mean you can't learn from your imperfections and be willing to make better stable choices.

Here's the thing, once you do wrong unintentionally, you're suppose to learn from it. This way the next time around, you'll know better than to entertain or partake in doing wrong willingly. Try not to use your imperfections as an excuse for you to bypass correction.

I know you're not perfect but that doesn't mean you can't at least strive to become. Learn and grow from your imperfections. Use your imperfections as a chance to change and be a better you, not for a chance to sit around, lack knowledge, and stay the same. You don't have to be perfect to know better, however, if you know better than do better.

There will always be a fight you have to face; however, victory belongs to Jesus. The battle is not yours.

Truth

For the word of God is alive and powerful. It is sharper than the sharpest two-edged sword, cutting between soul and spirit, between joint and marrow. It exposes our innermost thoughts and desires. -Hebrews 4:12

It amazes me how most people like to yell, "the devil is a lie! I rebuke you and that message from you. In the name of Jesus!" yet the whole time God sent the individual being rebuked to deliver the message. Before I proceed, I just want you to know that everything that hurt, doesn't mean it's not good for you, for example: The Truth.

When the Truth is spoken, you will know it because most people will start sweating, getting uncomfortable, offended, and very infuriated. They may even walk out the facility or walk away from you. It can get so bad that they may plot to try to kill you. Why? Because it pierced them and set something deep within them on fire that they're not ready to accept.

Overtime, they've became comfortable in their mess, lies, and deceived ways. It gets so bad that they become blinded and will try to argue with you over the truth that convicted them. The truth will forever speak for itself, so there's no need in arguing over it. However, these type of people claim to know the truth but get mad over it.

Truth of the matter is, they know what they want to know and anything outside of their misinterpretation and/or comfort zone is wrong.

For example: Just think about it, who do you know get mad at the Truth? One that's comfortable living a lie and not ready to accept it, right?

A lot of times, people will get mad at me for being truthful with them. They think I'm judging them or trying to provoke them to feel some type of way. Now, this is crazy and confusing to me because how do I know anyone inner secrets or thoughts. Here I am just being honest as I know how to be, and people hate it. Why? Because they don't understand the difference between conviction and condemnation.

If you ever happen to see someone run, avoid, hide, shame, argue, fight, and try to over talk someone else, regarding the Truth. Understand that they have a problem that only God can fix, if they allow him. They're just comfortable with prolonged dysfunction as they believe and continuously live deceived.

They think that conviction is the same as condemnation. They're unaware that when they feel convicted that's their opportunity to go to God and find out why.

For example: Just say you're having a normal conversation with someone and they say something to you that made you feel a certain way. It made you get angry and immediately throw a tantrum. What they said might've been something so simple that only needed a simple and calm response. However, something so simple irritated, offended, and made you feel guilty, for whatever reason. Now, whatever was said convicted you, which is why you felt some type of way. Conviction makes you feel uncomfortable but that's a good thing. Seeing that this happened, if you have a relationship with God, you should take what convicted you to him, to see what triggered the cake beneath all that icing. Once you find out the root of the matter, which could be hate, jealousy, anger, impatient, selfishness, insecurities, and/or pride; run to God immediately.

Whenever you feel convicted these are the steps you should take- Pray, Repent, confess, forgive yourself, turn away from it, learn, and grow from it. You should do these things immediately because if you don't, there's a possibility that you'll spend your life feeling and living condemned.

So now there is no condemnation for those who belong to Christ Jesus. And because you belong to him, the power of the life-living spirit has freed you from the power of sin that leads to death. The law of Moses was unable to save us because of the weakness of our sinful nature. So God did what the law could not do. He sent his Own Son in a body like the bodies we sinners have. And in that body God declared an end to sin's control over us by giving his Son as a sacrifice for our sins. He did this so that the just requirement of the law would be fully satisfied for us, who no longer follow our sinful nature but instead follow the Spirit. -Romans 8:1-4NLT

So, when you feel convicted, understand that it's the Truth piercing an area within you that needs to be confessed and set free. Whatever lives within your heart will be revealed one way or another. When it does, pray and confess that thing rapidly. Allow sanctification to have its way in your life.

The one who is confused and mislead, in most cases, came from one who is deceived and misinterprets. However, God is merciful and there's still Hope.

Pay people to not ask you for nothing

I know this may sound crazy but when you do it or if you've ever done it, you won't have any worries. People will have rough times, it doesn't matter how good of a job they have or what they may have in general. There will come a time, when someone need to borrow. There is nothing wrong with borrowing or loaning. However, you have a lot of selfish, shiesty, and greedy people in the world.

If they know you have it, they will say, do, and use whatever excuse they can to suck you dry and get it. So I say, pay people to not ask you for nothing. Money comes and go, it's a temporary piece of paper. However, this temporary piece of paper hold different amounts of value and power. People tend to go the extreme for it and about it.

Overtime, I realized that most people don't understand that if you do right by money, even though it's temporary, you will never run out of it. When you loan, borrow from, or give with right motives, you won't be infuriated by those with the wrong motives. This only happens when you understand the real meaning behind giving. I speak on giving in my book, "Erroneous Oracle" which will be releasing soon. However, lets move on. Money has a way of finding and chasing you. It has this unique way of surprising you.

When this happens, you will never run out of it. Now when you drain yourself by chasing it or trying to hold on to it, you will never have it. It will leave you so quick and have you wondering what just happened. Trying to find or chase it, is like chasing the wind, you'll never catch it to be able to secure it. Now I know I got a little carried away while speaking about money, but I wanted to give you an example regarding it before I proceed.

So I say, Pay people to not ask you for nothing. I know you're wondering what do I mean by that. Well, when someone try to be slick and leech off you, once you realize it, you don't have to entertain that negative energy anymore. You don't have to give another dollar to this individual, let them continue to use others, chase money that they'll never have, and be ungrateful. Don't get me wrong or don't get what I'm saying mixed up, there's nothing wrong with borrowing from, loaning, or giving.

However, you have to be careful where you plant seeds because you will either reap a fruitful harvest or a land of leeches. Don't be angry at all the money you given or all the times you tried to help others. That's their lost, not yours. It's their lost because they tried to take advantage of an opportunity to help better themselves. It's not your fought because your motives were right behind everything you've given and all the time you invested in trying to help them.

So that's why I say, Pay people to not ask you for nothing. This way if anything should ever happen, they will know that they can't get over on you anymore. I know that you don't mind giving or helping out, but you have to be careful because people will take your kindness as a weakness. So for now on, try to Pay people to not ask you for nothing else, however, don't stop giving, borrowing, and loaning because not everybody are leeches with the wrong motives.

Pray for others, don't prey on others.

Sweat

More than rare, I hear a lot of people saying, "Never let'em see you sweat". I ask myself why would numerous people say things like this? Is it because they're ashamed of what they've encountered throughout life? Is it because they're trying to maintain a certain look that doesn't require sweating? Maybe, it could be that they don't want to or can't handle the pressure that comes with/from sweating. There are probably numerous reasons as to why some people never want other people to see them sweat. Me personally, in my opinion, I think sweating is the most amazing thing ever. I like it because a lot of it comes out from you, with or without you realizing it. It relieves you and sometimes it relieves the people around you.

How does it relieve the people around you? It relieves them because when they see you sweat, they won't be ashamed to let others see them sweat.

For example: I'm sure you've been to some sort of workout facility before. You see some people that's there to workout but for some reason feel ashamed. It's quite difficult to understand because you and everyone else are pretty much there for the same reason, which is to workout. However, these people that are ashamed don't fully understand this. So, they stay out of the way and they don't exercise too much. Now you on the other hand, is just about everywhere, working out on every machine. You don't mind sweating, in fact, it looks as if someone poured a bucket of water on you because you're sweating so badly. However, not only are you sweating but your body is in shape, which is the way it needs to be. Now the person/people that is ashamed are watching. Some are learning and applying, while not being ashamed anymore and some are sitting around jealous and gossiping. Either way, you're not ashamed. Instead, you're focused and you're doing what you know is best for you with or without people watching.

Now with all this being said, I just want you to know that it's absolutely alright to always let'em see you sweat. Whether people see you sweat or not, they will always find a way to voice their twisted opinions regarding you and the things you do, good or bad. So, why not let'em see you sweat out that brokenness, that pride, that hurt, that unforgiveness, that toxic past, that negative mindset, and that rooted inner turmoil? Don't let nobody hinder you from breaking free and becoming a better person. They're only gossiping about you because they can't seem to understand how you manage to be courageous enough to standout and make better choices for yourself.

People or even you may say, "Never let'em see you sweat" but I say, "always let'em see you sweat"

It hurts to be quiet, yet everything doesn't require a response. It's worth remaining silent.

Never Say Never

I know that there's some things that you could never picture yourself doing, saying, or being apart of. However, you should never say what you'll never do, say, or what would never be you. More than rare, I hear a lot of people saying, "I'll never do that. Look at her, that'll never be me. Is he stupid? I would've never done anything like that" Now don't get me wrong there are numerous things people choose to do or they choose to not do. You either do it or you don't but never say never.

Believe it or not, you don't know what you'll find yourself doing or where you'll end up at in life. This explains why it's not safe to say what you'll never do or be. Once again, you either do it or you don't do it but never say never. I find that most people who say what they'll never do or be, are the ones who end up doing or being just that. The thing that gets me the most, is when they make themselves feel justified with numerous excuses as to why it's okay. This happens when they get caught in a act that they never thought they would someday be attached to or entertaining.

They also want those same people that they looked down on and said, "it could never be me" to spare compassion and be understanding. Now I'm not saying that people shouldn't have compassion and be understanding towards one another. What I'm saying is do to others, what you would want to be done to you. This is why I say you should never say never. Every day you wake up is a new day. That new day will hold new good things or new bad things. You may be placed in a situation where you have to make some tough decisions that you probably thought you would never have to make. You may find yourself experiencing something, similar to, that person you seen and said to yourself, "it could never be me"

Neither of us know what the day or our future holds. Due to us not knowing, we should pray, listen, and be understanding to others who may be experiencing a tough season. We shouldn't be bashing others, walking around full of pride like we can't be touched, and boasting about what would never happen to us. So, always remember to never say never.

When one is set free, another can be saved.

Accept Me

If you're alright with it, why do you need everyone to be alright with it? In this time of day, there are millions of people who do as they please. If they're born one way and they don't like it, they change themselves. If they enjoy getting high and drunk, they choose to make it a habit. If they enjoy cheating while married, being bi-sexual, a lesbian, and/or transgender, they do it. They have free will to do as they please. It's their life and their choices. However, free will is not the issue. The problem is when these type of people want everyone else to bow down, accept them, and the choices that they're making.

When I look around and see this dysfunctional, selfish, deceived, and confused behavior, I was left with no other thought then how unfair this is. I was just like wait a minute, you mean to tell me that I have to use my free will to bow down and accept you and the choices your making. Do we not all have free will?

For Example: I love shopping at Target. With my free will, I choose to shop at this store for everything. Now because I've become so comfortable to this store, it has led me to become completely deceived without me knowing it. Not only am I deceived, but I'm also very selfish. I feel like there's no need for other stores to exist. So, I gather with other Target shopping lovers and we all decide to pass a law that all other stores should be closed. Now we're all working hard to force others (including children) to agree and accept a choice that I made for me.

Would this be fair? ...No, Right? Why? Because for one, there are so many different stores to shop at. Two, not everyone like to shop at Target because it can be a bit pricey. Three, everyone has free Will to make their own choices in life. Hopefully, it's the right choices, but if not, that's their choice.

Before I proceed, I just want you to know that anyone who makes a choice to be and do as they please, yet needs to feel approved and accepted by others; aren't really happy, satisfied, or at peace with themselves or the choices that they're making. Now don't get me wrong, I Love everybody regardless of the choices that they make, however, there are boundaries that have been set. Just because I love you doesn't mean I have to accept and agree with every choice you make. Just like you choose to do as you please, I choose to love you from a distance and not partake, accept, or agree with the choices you choose to make.

Many people get offended by all the people who set boundaries. Not only do they get offended, but they'll start believing and yelling, "you're being judge-mental!" Now don't get me wrong some people are very judge mental but this is not always the case. More than rare, the individual is just offended and desires to be accepted. This explains why it's important to be careful with how you choose to live your life. If you're not happy with yourself and the choices you're making, why do you force others to accept you and those choices you're making?

As long as you're happy, satisfied, at peace with yourself and the choices you make, that's all that matters. Now when you start needing everyone else approval, acceptance, praise, and respect, something is wrong. This only shows how unhappy, unsatisfied, and miserable you are with yourself. To be completely honest with you, it doesn't matter how many people approve and accept you, if you don't love and accept yourself first, it will always be one thing after another, and you won't be satisfied. Why? Because that's an inner turmoil, deeply rooted that no man can fulfill.

The only time you feel you need to prove a point is when you've lost yourself.

Free Will

I choose to be me,

I choose to not allow anyone, or anything hinder me, Yes, I choose to be free.

I choose to live my life like Christ,

I choose to mediate, store, and abide by the Word of God and be a living sacrifice.

I choose to repent and turn away from sin,

I choose to let go of past hurt, confusion…move forward and start all over again.

I choose to live my life righteously,

I choose to love from a distance and stay away from manipulative people who finds pleasure in hypocrisy.

I choose to walk by faith and not by sight, even when my flesh and spirit is at war, I choose to seek God and remember victory belongs to Jesus, this is not my fight.

I choose to never force anyone to believe,

I choose to prepare and fulfill the Will of God, so when people are ready, they can willingly make a choice to be free and receive.

If what I choose makes anyone suffer or feel trapped, would that be fair? Would I be real in the decisions I choose to deal? This is why I don't get in the way of what others choose to do, Instead, I step aside and prepare the way so when they're ready, they can come through. Afterall, wouldn't that be the true definition of Free Will?

So, what do you choose to do? I would hope it's not to force others to use their free will to please a blind itch you can't even explain that lives within you.

Try not to speak negative on things and people that you still entertain and partake with.

Motivation

Just a couple of days ago my 5-year-old son asked me if he can use my phone to watch sketching videos on You tube. Now, my 10-year-old son is a great artist. It's like he was born with hands to draw. I realized at the age of 7, that drawing was his natural born gift from God.

Now due to my 5-year-old son father being absent in his life, he looks up to his older brother. Everything his older brother does motivates him. Now before I gave him my phone to get on you tube, I asked him a question. This question inspired me to produce and present this exhortation to you.

I asked him...Does your brother motivate you to find yourself and grow to be a better version of you? or does your brother motivate you to do everything he does and try to do it better? My son looked a bit puzzled with tears in his eyes. At that moment I realized that he wanted to be just like his brother to the point that he had forgotten his identity.

From there, I begin to encourage him by explaining to him how amazing he is. I told him that it's never too early or too late to find out who you are and to be a better person.

Moving forward, my baby inspired me to present this exhortation to you because I realized that he is not the only one who has gotten the real definition of motivation twisted.

Try not to lose yourself trying to be somebody else. I say this because most people look at motivation as competition. Instead of learning from the motivation, most people try to take it and use it against others or the ones who is trying to motivate them. When someone is equipped to motivate, inspire, influence, and encourage you naturally, don't wonder how and why God chose them. Instead accept and allow those tools to help you change, grow, and become a better version of yourself.

Don't get me wrong, there's nothing wrong with motivation. The problem occurs when you or others become jealous and envious of the motivation. The problem occurs when you or others turn the motivation into some type of race and/or competition. Normally this happens when the individual becomes frustrated trying to do something that was never assigned for them to do in the first place.

Let motivation do what it was designed to do, which is, motivating you to become a better version of you…not a better version of someone else. You were placed here on this earth temporary, for a reason. Allow motivation to help you find out and remember try not to lose yourself trying to be somebody else.

You first, have to prepare before you can serve.

Hate

When someone hate or is hating on you, 9 times out of 10 it's because they hate themselves. They don't feel like they're good enough. They struggle with trusting God and although they've given up on love, they need it more the same way we all need oxygen to breathe.

More than rare, people that hate others, strongly hate themselves based off past trauma that someone else has caused them. They beat and bash down themselves 1st, which causes them to feel selfless and worthless. They then, somehow gain many targets and murder them all one by one. When I say murder, I don't only speak on murdering an individual physically. I speak on murdering an individual verbally, mentally, and emotionally.

These people have a blind view and tend to see things out of eyes of envy, jealousy, and competition. There's still hope, however, they have to believe in order to properly receive healing. Because their view is blind, anyone they see, they assume that individual life is great, perfect, and better than theirs.

They don't fully comprehend that we all struggle with something and we all fall short. Most of us have our ways of covering up and making things look good on the outside. The hate is so strong in their heart, that damaging others and excluding their existence makes them feel secured on *the outside, yet they still struggle with finding peace, joy and freedom within.*

We all have a lot of hateful people among us. I'm sure it disgust, and hurt us when we hear all of their wrongdoings to innocent people who has done no harm to them. Instead of rejoicing to their sufferance of consequences, lets begin to pray for them every time we hear about another hateful act of theirs. Let us pray that God touch, heal, deliver, and forgive them. Let us pray that God grants them more of his Grace to grow, change, and learn from their wicked behaviors, choices, mistakes, and toxic past to become a better version of themselves.

Afterall, we do serve a mighty God who doesn't want anyone to perish but wants everyone to be redeemed and live a prosperous life for eternity. God has no favorites, which explains why he have mercy upon us all and grants us his Grace each day, he blesses us to see. People hate you because they first hate themselves. Instead of reacting out of ignorance, pray and allow love to be your reaction.

Always remember whatever is improperly installed will be produced improperly and affect many until repentance, forgiveness, healing, and deliverance takes place.

You're Amazing…Don't Give Up!

I Miss You

I'll never forget the day I got that call that stated you were gone, it felt as if my soul departed my body, instantly I grew weak feeling all alone.

I get so emotional when I go grocery shopping. As I walk down the aisle passing the cornstarch, my tears immediately appear, falling uncontrollably as I whisper to myself "It's going to be alright, not right now please don't start".

I have a couple of your blankets, covers, and pajamas. No matter how many times I wash them, I can never stop smelling your house scent, I know it's been a year and five months since you've left me, yet every day I wake up your death just seems so fresh and recent.

At times I wake up still hoping it's just a dream, every time someone speaks of you, my body shuts down and I silently begin to scream. I know I'm not crazy, I know I'm not the only one that feel this pain, I can't call you, I can't come to your house and everybody's acting like nothing happened....I'm trying to keep it together but Ma, I'm going insane.

One minute I'm crying, laying around, and questioning God about you, the next minute I'm smiling, moving forward, and living life the way you would want me to.

Everybody always say, "just think of the good memories of her", but they don't understand that I have so many of you that it causes my mind to blur. The only one that seems to stick the most is when I gave you a hug, told you I Love You, and kissed you; that was exactly 2 weeks before you permanently went ghost. I wish there was some way I can do those 3 things again, yet I can't and so I find myself writing about you again to simply say, "Ma, I really miss you."

Poetry By: Shamika King

Don't feel ashamed, worthless, hindered, and angry from a mortal rejection. Instead, rejoice and be glad because God has set you a part to be his reflection.

Demoralize

We live in a world, where people are praised, loved, and respected for doing wrong, yet beat down, looked at crazy, and disliked for doing right.

We live in a world, where people are afraid and cautious to help, yet bold enough to stand around, record, and watch when others get hurt.

We live in a world, where no one knows who they are, so they search for their identity in others, yet still find a way to hate on their sisters and brothers.

We live in a world, where people chase after what they want, yet grow impatient when it's time to pray, have faith, and go on an eternal hunt.

We live in a world, where people put on a mask and pretend just to keep up with the latest trend.

We live in a world, where people false advertise pure intentions for their own selfish reasons, fame, and a whole lot of attention.

We live in a world, where people turn away from the nourishing of the soul yet wouldn't mind sitting comfortable for years in a messy, miserable hole.

We live in a world, where people are fake and aren't fair, they always yelling, "When you fall down, I'll be there", yet later down the line, you find out there's only one who truly care.

We live in a world, where people desire to look and be what they see on tv or in the magazine, yet no matter how much money they spend to transition their bodies they still seem to suffer from insecurities and low self-esteem within.

We live in a world, where people pass corrupted laws and march through the streets to have it their way and be approved, yet when they go home behind closed doors, there's no peace and they still feel disapproved.

We live in a world, where people refuse to forgive and let go of their past, yet, get frustrated and wonder why they can never seem to undergo the same test in this life's class.

We live in a world, where mothers are selfish, children are rejected, and fathers are still a child living as a grown man, lost... roaming and dying in these streets thinking that's the only way to provide and be protective.

We live in a world, where there's too many lies and assumptions that no one could seem to be still, focus, and function. We may live in this world but that doesn't mean we have to be a part of its corrupted dysfunction. There's another way but are you ready to build and be a part of that eternal salvation?

Life is not so much about receiving blessings, it's about serving, giving, and being a blessing.

Don't Prove It

When you strive to be a better person each day, examine your heart and motives, you don't have to prove anything to anyone. As long as God knows, that's all that matters. Whatever you do privately will be revealed publicly. So, again you do not have to prove anything to anyone.

People will find a way to slander your name, whether you're doing good or bad. It doesn't matter how many times you try to explain. If they don't seek God for understanding, they won't understand anything you're draining yourself trying to explain.

If they haven't took the time to examine their heart, motives, and work on themselves within, it's pointless trying to explain or even have a conversation with them. To be honest, you have no business trying to prove yourself to a mortal in the first place.

If you're doing what you know is the right thing to do in the sight of our Lord and savior, Jesus Christ, you're going to be just fine without the approval of others. You have no business seeking validation from others and proving points. If you do, you'll find that it's impossible and draining to please and satisfy people who already has their mind made up regarding you.

Sometime people are so wrapped up in bondage, pain, misery, and unforgiveness, that their view is blinded. They tend to speak towards you based off what they suffer from within themselves. Many times, they like to play the victim and make everything about you and what you say is evil.

Now by the Grace of God, there's still hope for people like this to repent, turn away from sin, and seek God wholeheartedly for a pure heart, understanding, and discernment. However, until then don't waste your energy and time trying to prove anything to mortals. The only time you feel the need to prove yourself is when you don't feel like you're enough.

You desire for others to like, believe, and trust in you so that you can feel content, and complete about yourself. Not only that but you want to feel in control. When things don't go your way, anything people say or do may infuriate and irritate you. If this is you, I encourage you to examine yourself and seek God to find out why do you react this way and why do you desperately need praise and approval from others.

When you grow to know who God created you to be, you begin to understand that the only one who you owe an explanation to about anything that you do is God alone. So, when people come to bash and slander you, you'll know not to prove anything.

After all, actions speak louder than words. If they refuse to see the God in you, what makes you think they're going to listen and accept the God that speaks through you. Whatever you do, don't prove it. Allow the way you live to be all the proof they'll ever receive without you having to utter word.

Sometimes when you meet people you may see only two colors...white or black. However, if you stick around long enough their true colors will be revealed.

Not on my level

When I'm out and about, it amazes me how prideful and prejudice most people can be. I watch as they sit on their high horses and look down on others who they feel are below them. Most of them think that because they graduated with every degree a university could offer and have the highest paying career on the market, that they're better, smarter, and wiser than others.

Most of them think that because they're a home or building owner and ride in a foreign car, that they're better, smarter, and wiser. Most of them think that because they've raced to achieve whatever they desired first, they're better, smarter, and wiser.

I can go on and on about these type of people, but I've decided not to hold you up and get right to the point. I'm not sure about you but as I observe these types of people, I realized that they have no morals.

They don't listen or respect anyone. They are very impatient and if you asked them what real joy is, they'd probably mock you. They're not organized nor are they clean. They procrastinate about everything, very lazy, and always find a quick plot to get more of everything, not just money.

They are greedy, selfish and never fully satisfied with anything. They have no peace, always on the go, can't focus, and isn't content. They're slow to listen, and quick to get offended and angry. In their minds you're never enough and you'll always be disqualified.

If you're not on their level or where they feel you should be, you'll never be nothing or achieve anything in life. However, let's just say you're the type to strive to compete and be like others and you do make it to their level, they'll still be suspicious of you. They'll still hate, mock, betray, and use you.

They'll still find a way to bash, slander, and devour you. They'll take credit for everything you worked hard for, boast about it, and call it theirs. I'm here to inspire you to continue growing and becoming a better you. Stay away from anyone who acts, thinks, and feel that they're better, smarter, and wiser.

We are all equal. It doesn't matter what race or color you are. It doesn't matter where you live or where you work. It doesn't matter if you're rich or poor. It doesn't matter what type of car you have, how much money, and degrees you have.

We are all equal human beings. We may be different, but we all have a lot in common. Just because a person makes an extra dollar, have a bit more space in their house and drive an updated car, doesn't make them higher or better. I find that when you say this to people who feel you're not on their level, they get very infuriated and offended...why? Because they refuse to believe it's true. They'd rather believe money and the materialistic items that they worked hard for, defines their character.

Again, we are all equal, and I don't say this to make anyone feel justified, I say it because it's the truth. Just like we all were born on an unexpected day and time. We all can die on an unexpected day and time. We're all just borrowing this body suit and renting a place in this world temporarily. So, in this case, the cares of this world and this body shouldn't cause us to get beside ourselves, boast, and turn our nose up towards anyone. What really matters is our soul and spirit, in which can live on for eternity, if we feed it more than we feed our flesh. So, why not boast about that? Why not nourish and work hard to build that? Why not purify the heart and renew the mind, daily? Why not have patience and strive each day to examine and feed that?

Just as fast as you make it to the top and gain the desires of this world, you can hit rock bottom and lose everything even faster. The people you once mocked due to them not being on your level, will be the same ones you'll find yourself serving and gaining knowledge from.

With that being said, whatever level you're on, stay right there. Take your time and gain the knowledge, wisdom, and understanding of God. Practice and apply morals; after all, it's free. I mean I know people try to pay for what comes free, but it never works, why? Because it's nothing like going to the creator for healing instead of the creation.

Life is not a race, it's marathon which means you can take as much time as you need to get everything about yourself together, starting within first. Whatever season or level you're on, again stay right there. Learn, grow, examine yourself, and change for the better. Every time you grow from a season, reach out and help lift-up others that may be in need, don't look down on them.

Don't ever forget where you come from and I don't say this to make you feel hindered. I say this so that you can remember to help others who may be less fortunate, whenever you have the chance, instead of looking down on them being greedy, prideful, and selfish. Keep your distance from people that think highly of themselves. Don't be deceived and don't try to get to where they are. Remain humble, content, and have patience. Never look down on anyone, and never forget…. we are all equal.

Repent, forgive yourself, and leave it alone.

Trust

I remember a couple of years ago when I was a part of an anti-Christ ministry ran by a false prophetess and elder. When I first met these people, they came off very generous and loving. I was on a mission to get to know God and live my life like Christ. I was like a newborn baby in Christ, I wasn't sure where to start. Instead of praying to God, I placed my trust in these people to guide me.

Little by little, I shared information that I would've never shared with anyone. I placed my trust in them to teach me the Word of God. I placed my trust in them to the point where I begin to draw closer to them and what they said, instead of God. I drew so close to them that I drew further away from God. To be honest, I never even got a chance to spend any time with God because these people were very needy and controlling.

After about 2 ½ years, I realized that things weren't getting any better, but even worse. I still felt drained and chained. I started to seek God first without them knowing and the truth about who they really were, was revealed. I, then, decided to leave their false kingdom that had nothing to do with God. However, after leaving I was worse off than before I started. I was even more hurt, bitter, angry, and unforgiving.

I wanted revenge and I refused to forgive them. It was so bad that I was either going to kill them or commit suicide. I was left all alone feeling worthless. These erroneous oracles used and abandoned me just like everyone else that I placed my trust in. However, little did I know my life was just beginning.

The sacrifice you desire is a broken spirit. You will not reject a broken and repentant heart, O God. -Psalms 51:17 NLT

Moving forward, as I grew to know God, I learned that I had no business trusting in mortals. I learned that the one I should be trusting is God and God alone. Overtime, I learned and realized that this is why I was so hurt, bitter, angry, and unforgiving all the time.

Trusting in mortals will always leave you wrapped in bondage. Why? Because people change. Just like faith moves God, feelings move people. One day they like you the next day, week, or year they hate you. One day they're understanding, the next day, week, or year, they're unforgiving. One day they're faithful, honest, and consistent, the next day, week, or year they're cheating, lying, and procrastinating.

One day they're transparent about everything, the next day, week, or year the refuse to communicate. One day they're with you, the next day, week, or year they leave you for whatever reason. One day they're making promises, the next day, week, or year they're breaking promises. One day they're loving and trustworthy, the next day, week, or year they're draining, envious, and can't be trusted.

This can be anyone such as; family, friends, co- workers, children, parents, husband, wife, neighbors, and strangers. Whoever or whatever it may be, do not trust it.

Don't trust anyone-not your best friend or even your wife. -Micah 7:5NLT

Again, this explains why many people are hurt, angry, bitter, unforgiving, and hindered. They trust in mortals, that not only do all the things I just spoke about, but they can be here physically in this body suit one minute and wiped clean from the earth the next day, week, or year.

I am writing to encourage and inspire you to Trust God. When you trust God, you won't have to worry about being heart broken, hurt, bitter, and unforgiving. You won't have to worry about God abandoning you. You will be at peace and you will know how to guard your heart at all times.

You will keep in perfect peace all who trust in you, all whose thoughts are fixed on you. -Isaiah 26:3NLT

God would never do to you what mortals do to you. I'm sure I'm not the only one who had to learn the hard-hurtful way. However, if God has mercy for me, he'll have mercy for you. If Jesus guided me and remained faithful by my side, he'll do the same for you. There's still hope, however, be willing to Trust God first no matter what.

Trust in the Lord with all your heart; do not depend on your own understanding. Seek his Will in all you do, and he will show you which path to take. -Proverbs 3:5-6NLT

The choices that people make are completely out of your reach. Do what you know is the right thing to do and stop allowing people to define and control your character.

Victim

Before you get comfortable with someone, set aside plenty of time to get to know them as much as possible. As you grow to know them, do not bypass what they say and/or do. Pay close attention to how they treat, speak, and act with you and others. If they're gossiping about others to you, please know that they will gossip about you to others.

When they talk, vent, or gossip be very quiet and listen. One thing that I've learned is that when you're quick to listen and slow to speak, you'll find out more than you expected, without having to ask. To spot an individual that plays the victim is not hard at all. Again, if you listen carefully and pay close attention to their actions, you will know exactly whose pretending and who is real.

I would like to give you 12 characteristics of an individual who plays the victim but really is a wolf in sheep clothing.

1.   They come off very sweet, charming, innocent, loving, and caring. They know just what to say to get you to submit and draw close to them.

2.   They'll have your back a 100 percent. They will also stand by your side, as long as it doesn't have anything to do with them.

3.   They will not take full responsibility for their actions. If they're wrong about something, they will not apologize. They will place the blame on you or someone else. They also love all of the fame.

4.   *They are very selfish, greedy, and are never satisfied. They hate giving, however, be careful because they are great actors. They act like they love to give but they don't. They'll say, "Yes, sure I got it" but behind closed doors they'll say, "I shouldn't give them anything. They don't do nothing for me". No matter what you do, it will never be good enough to them, (remember they're greedy) They'll mock you and say, "You think you doing something. This ain't nothing, I could or could've done it better".*

5.   *When any form of pressure or trouble come, they will run to save themselves. As long as they're safe and sound that's all that matters. Don't bother looking for them because they won't be anywhere in sight at least until things cool down.*

6.   *If you ever confront them about something that they've done wrong, get ready for them to cause a scene. I mean they will cry, loud talk you, throw shade, want to fight or harm you, and slander your name. Be careful because some of them will remain calm as if nothing happened. Even if you approach them in a respectful way, they will panic as if you're the bad one trying to harm them.*

7.   *They are great liars and table-turners. They will lie to make themselves look good and convince others to be on their side. They will also lie to make a good person look or seem suspicious/evil. They will flip the script so good and Smoove, that they will have you thinking you're the crazy one.*

8.   *They will stay away from you, turn others against you, and secretly watch your every move. It can be someone in your family, at work, friends, neighbors, or even someone at church. If you know who they really are, and they know you know the truth about them. They will try to turn almost everyone against you. If not them, they will manipulate and use others to watch you and collect any kind of information from you, only to use it against you. They love to say, "See, I told you so. You need to leave alone/stay away from him/her. They're crazy and I wouldn't want you to get involved in their evil doings". However, it's them that has many vicious secrets and if you talk to someone*

else, they're afraid that you'll have a chance at finding out the truth about them.

9.   *They love attention, are very prideful, and controlling. Although they act like the don't, these people LOVE attention. They are very manipulative, it's their way or the highway. Tell them NO and watch how all hell break loose. They will bring everything they've ever done for you and use it all against you to make you feel bad enough to give them what they want. Remember, they're very selfish. They also love drama and they gossip about others only to make themselves look good.*

10. *They'll call you out to shame you, yet they'll never admit to anything that they've done. I'm not sure if I can stress this enough but remember these people are selfish. They feed off any kind of attention even if that means they have to slander and/or bash you.*

11. *They are one-sided, close minded individuals. They know what they know, and you can't tell them anything. These are the type of people that you have to let keep hitting a brick wall. As crazy as it sounds, they will get mad and offended if you tell them something that they didn't know or if you do something without informing them first.*

12. *They like to be and do everything first. They're very jealous and competitive individuals. Again, these are very selfish, greedy, and prideful people. They will secretly watch and rob others of any and everything, then, come out as if they were the first to do it. It doesn't matter what it is, if you go to school, they'll find a quicker way to go to school and graduate in the same field first. If you're getting ready to get married, before you know it, they'll be getting married too. If you're trying to become a home or building owner, before you know It, they'll be doing it too. Again, they'll take what you do, make it theirs, and convince themselves/others that they can do it better.*

Now these were just a couple of characteristics. There may be more that I haven't learned or experienced yet. The list can go on and on. However, I just wanted to bring it to your attention so that you can be mindful and aware of these people. At some point you may wonder what causes people to play the victim. I've learned overtime that people like this has allowed there past hurt and unforgiveness to rot within them, in which, was caused by someone else. It could be things such as rejection from a parent, molestion by a stranger or family member, or simply not enough love and attention from mortals.

Due to these people refusing to repent, forgive, let it go, and seek God for healing and deliverance, they suffer and play the victim throughout their life, no matter the situation. Again, I just wanted to help you be aware and guard your heart from people like this. If you're not careful, you'll find yourself walking around playing the victim as well. Always remember that hurt people, hurt people. The infections of a prolonged, open painful wound spreads like a disease and before you know it, you'll find yourself caught up in that sickness, if you're not careful.

What you choose to do, is what YOU choose to do. It shouldn't be based off past hurt, rejection, lack of attention, love, and affection or whatever someone else has done to you. Stop making up excuses as to why you refuse to repent, forgive yourself, others, and be set free from bondage.

No

In this time of age, you will rarely hear anyone tell someone No. Reason being is because no one wants to offend anyone. No one wants to cause anyone to feel rejected. Believe it or not, even the one who is always saying Yes doesn't want to be told No.

I know what it feels like to be emotionally abandoned, rejected, and told No. When I first began to experience these things, I was angry and broken. I couldn't believe that certain people that I was there for, had the nerve to tell me No. I learned later in my days that it's never who you think will be there for you, it's always somebody that you would least expect.

I was never the type to give someone something and expect something back from them. When I told someone Yes, I looked at whatever I was giving as a lost. If I got it back, I got it back, if not, then ok. Due to me being human, It still lingered in my mind who can I count on to be there for me and why do I feel a certain way when someone tell me No.

After spending alone with God and meditating on his Word, I learned even more about myself. I learned that the only one I can truly count on is Jesus. I learned that the reason I felt a certain way when someone told me No is because I didn't forgive my mother for emotionally abandoning and rejecting me. I also learned that I wanted to be approved by mortals who can disqualify and disapprove me at any given moment.

Once I learned these things about myself, I repented, confessed, and surrendered it all to God. Since then, I've humbled myself. When someone tells me No, whether their being selfish or simply just can't do it, I still thank them, and I remain content. I am writing to encourage you to do the same if you feel convicted, ashamed, rejected, or disqualified when someone tell you No.

It can be a No from your parents, best friend, husband, wife, children, or a certain job. The moment you feel offended and start to get infuriated, calm down. Respond respectfully and go home. When you get home, pray and ask God what is it that's rooted in your heart to cause you to feel such way the moment someone tell you No.

Too many people are saying and hearing Yes, to the point where it causes conflict when someone says No. Due to people looking to other people to validate them, they feel disqualified and worthless when people say No. What is Jesus saying? What does Jesus think about you? To be honest, God doesn't always say Yes. There has been plenty of times God told me, "No, wait or No, leave that alone, or No, not yet."

If God always told me Yes, how could I ever learn to be patience and humble myself? I wouldn't even know what faith is. I would panic every time something occurs, and I would never be able to endure. I would run from any kind of pressure that's needed for me to grow, learn, and change. In fact, I would always have it my way and I wouldn't even need Jesus by my side.

Do you see how much conflict it causes when you always say Yes? Sometimes you have to say No just because. Not to be mean or selfish but to move out of people way, so that they can at some point stop seeking you and start seeking God for everything they need. Now don't get me wrong you may have it, but you should take care of yourself. You should be a good steward over what God has blessed you with.

If you're not careful, people will take your Yes as your weakness and suck you dry. If you ever told them No, they'll blame their root of rejection, poor choices, and lack of responsibility on you. They may even bring up everything they've ever done for you since you've been alive. Don't feel bad and get all vulnerable. They only react this way for 3 reasons;

1. They fear rejection from mortals, and they don't know that they're always qualified by Jesus even when he says No.

2. Due to you always saying Yes, they've made you an Idol in their life and expect you to provide their every need.

3. They suffer from some sort of past hurt and rejection from someone else and refuse to seek God for understanding and healing.

I challenge you to practice saying No more often. Some people will hate you and some will appreciate you. Either way, you'll save a lot of people lives and you'll be at peace with your own.

You'll never know what you can do until you have patience, focus, humble yourself, and draw close to the one in whom created you (God)

Challenge

I challenge you to wake up, repent, confess your sins, and pray each day.

I challenge you to live your life like Christ, serve, and give each day.

I challenge you to smile every day.

I challenge you to have patience and respond in a calm way, no matter the situation.

I challenge you to hold the door or elevator open for someone.

I challenge you to apologize even if it wasn't your fault.

I challenge you to give someone a hug that you don't know and tell them it's going to be alright.

I challenge you to forgive someone that hurt you and let it go.

I challenge you to write a mini inspiring note to someone you don't know.

I challenge you to say Thank You, Sorry, and/or Excuse me as much as possible.

I challenge you to give up your seat to a child, expecting mother, disabled person, or an elder man/woman.

I challenge you to treat others how you would want them to treat you or those dear to your heart.

I challenge you to buy someone breakfast, lunch, or dinner today.

I challenge you to help someone in any way you can today.

I challenge you to not allow anyone steal your joy today.

I challenge you to say something nice to someone you don't know today.

I challenge you to give someone you don't know something priceless today.

I challenge you to not get wrapped up in or listen to any drama today.

I challenge you to put your phone down, shut all devices off and spend time with your loved ones. (Play a board game or something).

I challenge you to put your phone on DND and do something for yourself, by yourself (even if it's just taking a little nap, reading your favorite book, or watching a movie you never watched before)

I challenge you to cook something you never cooked before.

I challenge you to not worry about anything today, just let this day play itself out.

I challenge you to laugh more and cry as much as you need to.

I challenge you to not respond to anything negative and always keep a positive energy.

I challenge you not to yell or use profanity today.

I challenge you to drink more water and eat something healthy each day.

I challenge you to stop being indecisive and buy something nice for yourself.

I challenge you to be you and stop trying to fit in or keep up with others.

I challenge you to keep moving forward and no matter what never give up. There's still hope, and you matter.

I challenge you to take an extra snack, water, or lunch, to work and share it with your co-worker.

I challenge you to look at yourself in the mirror and say something amazing to yourself before you leave the house.

I challenge you to be quick to listen and slow to speak, even if you have a lot to say.

I challenge you to not argue with others over anything.

I challenge you to have patience and self-control.

I challenge you to stop trying to prove everything to mortals.

I challenge you to love yourself.

I challenge you to think before you react/respond.

I challenge you to be quiet if you don't have anything nice or truthful to say.

I challenge you to seek God when you feel convicted.

I challenge you to always have something ready to give the homeless. (It doesn't have to always be money. It can be fruit, food, a gift card, or a bottle of water) Anything will help.

I challenge you to face and examine yourself each day.

I challenge you to learn, grow, change, and be a better person each day.

I challenge you to pull over and help someone with a flat tire or give someone a jump. (Be careful while doing so)

I challenge you to give someone a ride to the train or to a safe and close by bus station.

I challenge you to tell someone you love them.

I challenge you to ask someone about their day and listen.

I challenge you to buy someone a coffee or tea.

I challenge you to let someone in line get in front of you to check-out first.

I challenge you to take a day and just get you some rest. (Call off work if you need to)

I challenge you to trust God to provide all your needs and stop worrying.

Use each day to spread Love and Inspire those you know and don't know freely. You don't have to do it all in one day. Do what you can, when you have the opportunity. Don't wait for someone to ask you. A lot of people are too prideful, overly independent, or simply afraid of rejection. Be a blessing unexpectedly. Don't wait around for a thank you or broadcast what you do for others. Do it as if you're doing it unto our heavenly Father.

If you can think of any other ways to spread Love and Inspire others, please don't hesitate to do so.

What affects one Temple will most certainly affect another Temple…So, be honest with yourself and get yourself together first.

Boundaries

Whoever has no rule over his own spirit is like a city broken down, without walls. -Proverbs 25:28 NKJV

Boundaries are a powerful weapon. When you set them, they won't only protect you, but they'll help you gain self-control. I challenge you to understand your worth as a woman or man. Set you some boundaries and stand on them, no matter what. From experience, I can assure you that you will be at peace.

Many people will know not to come near you. In fact, you'll begin to isolate yourself, cut a lot of people off, or they'll leave on their own. Why? Because of your boundaries. Also, because they won't be able to come, go, control, and do as they please with you.

When you set boundaries prepare yourself for tons of backlash. People will slander your name, call you crazy, use your past against you, and spread false accusations about you. I am writing to encourage you to not be moved or discouraged by this if it happens.

Again, they only do this because you're choosing to better yourself. They can choose to do the same for themselves, but they chose not to. They can't seem to understand why you're choosing to set boundaries and to be honest, they don't care. They just want to be able to do as their selfish flesh desires when it come to you and they want you to tolerate it.

Setting boundaries won't be easy but it will be worth it. Distractions and temptations will forever surround you but when you know your worth and set boundaries, it won't have an affect on you like it did before. Set yourself some boundaries, stand on them no matter what it is or who it is, and guard your heart.

You're not missing out on anything. What's for you has been set aside just for you…So, take your time.

Shut Up!

But when thou doest alms, let not thy left hand know what thy right hand doeth. -Matthew 6:3 KJV

If you're in a relationship...Shut up!

If you're engaged or getting ready to get married...Shut up!

If you're getting ready to buy a house or own property for the first, second or third time...Shut up!

If you're getting ready to purchase a new or used car...Shut up!

If you're getting ready to have your 1st, 2nd, 3rd, or 4th baby...Shut up!

If you're getting ready to move out of town or within town...Shut up!

If you got hired at a new job or got a raise...Shut up!

If you're getting ready to make a change or do something new...Shut up!

If things happen to not go as you expected relationship or marriage wise, or in general...Shut up!

Whatever the accomplishment, failure, or complaint may be...Shut up!

*Now I'm not saying walk around as if you're perfect and flawless. Neither am I saying look down on others. I'm simply saying **STOP RUNNING YOUR MOUTH!** Get rid of that root of pride and seek God to find out why that heart of yours seeks praise, approval, and attention from others. There are many people that you know or unaware of, that watches your every move. They will be proud of you one day to your face. They will be jealous of you and slander your name, the next day behind your back.*

Most times you may wonder, why does nothing never work out for you? or why can't you seem to get important things done? Truth be told, it's because you run your mouth too much and you use a lot of your time trying to prove what you run your mouth about.

Here's the thing, the more you run your mouth, the more you're going to have to prove yourself. The more you try to prove yourself, the more drained, stressed, confused, and depressed you'll find yourself. Again, whatever the accomplishment, failure, or complaint may be...Shut up!

I am writing to encourage you to get whatever it is done in silence. When it's done, send out invitations and whoever show up will know. In the meantime, Shut up!

Check the root before you enter that garden and fall for the servings of its fruit.

No one can use anything against you when you don't have anything to hide or be ashamed of.

What use to be doesn't still have to be.

For example: Your past and everything about it.

Let it go.

Special letter to Readers

Thank you for your patience and time that you've set aside to read this book. I pray that the Nourish Inspirations that I've served you, encourages you to become a better person. I pray that it pierced and motivated you to seek God for yourself. Jesus Christ is the only one who can truly lead and redeem you. I am just a servant of Jesus that's been placed here to feed you.

After breakfast Jesus asked Simon Peter, "Simon son of John, do you love me more than these? "Yes, Lord," Peter replied, "you know I love you." "Then feed my lambs," Jesus told him.

Jesus repeated the question: Simon son of John, do you love me?" "Yes, Lord," Peter said, "you know I love you." "Then take care of my sheep," Jesus said.

A third time he asked him, "Simon son of John, do you love me?" Peter was hurt that Jesus asked the question a third time. He said, "Lord, you know everything. You know that I love you." Jesus said, "Then feed my sheep.

-John 21:15-17 NLT

May God continue to bless and be with you.

Contact Information

Listen to my podcast at your convenience and be inspired.

Podcast: Anchor.fm/nourishinspirations

<u>Other Books by Shamika King</u>

Face Yourself

But God Kept Me

What They Can't See Affects Them

*All books are available on **amazon.com/author/shamikaking***

Dedication

This book is dedicated to all of the
mothers who have lost a child in anyway.

Foreword

October 12, 2001. That was the day I lost a piece of my heart. I was twenty-four years old, just getting to know this thing we call life. I was a mother of two boys and engaged to the person who I thought I was going to spend the rest of my life with. I was young, and what some might call 'wet behind the ears.' I thought I had everything figured out. I thought I was making the right decisions for my children; but really, I wasn't.

"I'm sorry; there was nothing else we could do." Those are the words that no mother ever wants to hear. The walls seemed to be caving in. I felt weak; like my body was going to collapse. My first thought was that this must be a dream, this cannot be true. I need to see my son. But it was true. My one-year old son was gone just like that; just a month after we celebrated his birthday. And what made it even worse, he was taken at the hands of then "fiancée." I blamed myself for so long. I left my sons that morning with my fiancé. I was so excited that I was starting

a new job that day. I never imagined that the day would end the way that it did. And instead of blaming the person that had taken my son's life; I blamed myself.

How are you supposed to cope after losing a child? How can you continue to live life as usual? How can you wake up every day knowing your child is gone? What did I do to deserve this? Why can I not carry a child?

These are all questions that a mother goes through in her mind when she loses a child. There is no other feeling that can cut you to your core. No one can say anything to make it better.

In this book I will go through what you may experience during this time of loss. Through my experience when I lost my children. Whether it be through miscarriage, or death, whether natural or at the hands of another person. Although you will never get over the pain of losing a child, you can learn to heal from the pain, one day at a time, through faith and prayer.

Table of Contents

Chapter 1: Giving Life 1

Chapter 2: I'm Sorry 6

Chapter 3: The 5 Stages of Grief 9

Chapter 4: Where do I go from here 34

Intro: Blessing from God

Then the people brought their little children to Jesus so that he could lay his hands on them to bless them and pray for them. When the followers saw this, they told the people to stop bringing their children to him. But Jesus said, "Let the little children come to me. Don't stop them, because God's kingdom belongs to people who are like these little children." After Jesus blessed the children, he left there. Matthew 19 13:15ERV

Chapter 1

Giving Life

"When a woman gives birth to a baby, she has pain, because her time has come. But when her baby is born, she forgets the pain. She forgets because she is so happy that a child has been born into the world."
– John 16:21 ERV

Do you remember giving birth? The pain you endured, then in a blink of an eye, this beautiful child was laid on your chest. You count each of those tiny toes and remember the way he/she opened their eyes for the first time and connected with yours. The tears of joy you shed while saying, "You're the most beautiful baby in the world." Those are the precious moments when your child enters the world, and memories that will stay with you for the rest of your life.

But what if that time was brought on with immediate loss? What if your child was still born? I had a friend who went through this. I was called immediately to the hospital when the baby was born. My

friend was so strong. As I was driving on the way to the hospital, all I could think about was my son. I had lost him three months prior. I knew my friend needed my support and that's why I was called; but I had no idea what to say to her. I never experienced a still born child. I told myself that my friend needed me to help her get through a time such as this, and the fact that I myself had lost a child would help me be able to help her. As I entered the room. my friend was sitting on the bed, holding her little girl. The way she caressed her hair and tiny little fingers, I couldn't do anything but console her. The first thing I said besides me being sorry, was, "don't worry. We don't know why these things happen; but I am going to be with you to help you through it." I will never forget that day.

Being a mother is the greatest feeling in the world, knowing that you now have this tiny person who is dependent on you. It can be joyful and scary all at the same time. It's not easy being a mother; but you learn as you go. And with each child you learn different things.

In the next pages, write down the first memory you have of giving birth to your child. The way he/she looked, the pain, your emotions of how you felt. Write as if you're telling your child the first moments of his/her life and the feelings you had. Even if your child was still born, write your feelings.

When You Were Born...

_____
_____
_____
_____
_____
_____
_____
_____
_____
_____
_____
_____
_____
_____
_____
_____
_____
_____
_____
_____
_____
_____

_____
_____
_____
_____
_____
_____
_____
_____
_____
_____
_____
_____
_____
_____
_____
_____
_____
_____
_____
_____
_____
_____
_____
_____
_____
_____

Chapter 2
I'm Sorry

"I'm sorry. There's nothing more we could do."

This is the moment you find out your child is gone. It feels like you're in a movie, and it's all in slow motion. That's how I felt when I was told my child was gone. I could see the time he was born, and all his most memorable moments flashed before my eyes. The pain I felt in my heart was like no other, period. It was as if this was a joke; but who would joke about something like this? Am I asleep? This must be a dream; but I pinch myself and I can feel it.

What do I do? how do I get to my child? Maybe if I just hold him, he will come back. I hold his hand, nothing happens. He's still warm. I know there's life in him. I know he's there. I know he can hear me. "Why don't you wake up? I don't understand?" My heart is beating feels like a thousand times a minute. Every nerve in my body is shaking. I'm

there physically; but mentally, I'm slowly fading away.

This is one moment, besides the birth of your child, that you will never forget. There is nothing at this time that anyone can say or do, to make you feel any better, period. This is your baby, your child, that you have carried in your womb; whether it was full term or a couple weeks, you still had a connection.

Sometimes when I hear people say, "oh, she lost her child. She was only a couple weeks into her pregnancy. Luckily it happened now rather than later." Really? I never understand how people think that losing a child in the womb, is any different from losing a child that's outside the womb. You still have lost a child, and you still love that child unconditionally; whether you have physically given birth, or the baby passed in the womb.

The moment you find out that there's a baby growing inside, you start to eat different, act different, and even look different. You start to rub your belly daily and make plans Spreading the news with loved ones is a joy. But now that is all

gone, since your baby, your child, has passed.

Prayer: Lord, please come in my time of need. I am lost and don't know which way to turn or what to do at this time.

"Chills, I am shaking from head to toe. I see doctors, nurses and others coming into the room. I feel pins and needles in my hands and feet. This can not be true, this is deceit. I look at your face, there is no expression. You lay in the bed like you're sound asleep. I touch your hand, it's still warm. 'Come back, come back,' I whisper in your ear. 'Don't be afraid; mommy is here.' As the doctors pull me away, I know it's true; my baby is gone now. What am I going to do?"

Chapter 3

The 5 Stages of Grief & Loss
1. **Denial & Isolation.**
2. **Anger.**
3. **Bargaining.**
4. **Depression.**
5. **Acceptance.**

As you know there are five stages of grief. You might not go through every stage, but you will at least go through two or three. Some people say you go through all and you don't even notice it. The number of stages you go through really depends on the person. I personally went through all. In the next couple pages, we're going to dive into all five stages, so that you can define and understand what you're going through and why.

After each stage, I will give examples of my experience, then you can write how you may have gone through the same thing.

Sonya Johnson

Denial

Denial is a common defense
mechanism that buffers the immediate
shock of the loss, numbing us to our
emotions. We block out the words and
hide from the facts. We start to believe
that life is meaningless, and nothing is of
any value any longer. For most people
experiencing grief, this stage is a
temporary response that carries us
through the first wave of pain.

Axelrod, J. (2018). The 5 Stages of Grief &
Loss. Psych Central. Retrieved on October 30,
2018, from https://psychcentral.com/lib/the-5-
stages-of-loss-and-grief/

This stage is usually expressed at the
onset of finding out that your child has
passed away. YOU are in denial. You say
to yourself. "No, this cannot be true; this
is a nightmare. They have the wrong
person." You are numb to your emotions
at this time. You're wondering, how am I
going to go on? Can I go on? Is it possible
for me to get through this?

This is all normal. Now the question
at hand is how to move on. This stage may
last as long as one day, a week, or even

longer. It depends on the person. I believe I was in denial for the first week. I kept saying to myself that this was all a sick joke. At night I would lay in the bed and see my child laying in that hospital bed. I would imagine him coughing and waking up, and the hospital staff running to the room. I would wait to hear the phone ring at my parents' house, telling me it's a miracle, he is here. He's alive. As we know, that call never came. This also was the beginning of my isolation stage. Denial leads to Isolation, in which I know all too well. The period where you don't want to talk, see or have interaction with anyone.

I would lay in the bed most of the day, numb. I didn't care about eating, seeing family. I used to ask myself, "why am I here, and you're not." The world was meaningless to me, nothing at that moment was important anymore.

I went through the same emotions during my miscarriages. I kept saying, "the ultrasound is wrong, maybe they missed it." I suffered two miscarriages in my life. I didn't go through the denial stage with the first one. The second, I did.

I knew from what was happening based on what was going on with my body, but I acted like it wasn't. I ignored the signs. In my mind, if I don't address it, it's not happening. When me and my husband did go to the ER, the ultrasound showed what deep down I already knew.

We deny what we don't want to believe.

On the following lines, describe when you think you used denial. When did you realize the truth?

Denial_____

_____

_____

_____

_____

_____

_____

_____

_____

_____

_____

_____

_____

_____

_____

_____

_____

_____

_____

_____

_____

_____

_____

Sonya Johnson

_____

_____

_____

_____

_____

_____

_____

_____

_____

_____

_____

_____

_____

_____

_____

_____

_____

_____

_____

_____

_____

_____

_____

_____

_____

_____

Anger

As the masking effects of denial and isolation begin to wear, reality and its pain re-emerge. We are not ready. The intense emotion is deflected from our vulnerable core, redirected and expressed instead as anger. The anger may be aimed at inanimate objects, complete strangers, friends or family.

Axelrod, J. (2018). The 5 Stages of Grief & Loss. Psych Central. Retrieved on October 30, 2018, from https://psychcentral.com/lib/the-5-stages-of-loss-and-grief/

Anger. You may be angry with everyone. If you're married, you will express that anger towards your husband. You may be angry with members of your family. Everyone will feel like an enemy. You may even be angry at your child that passed on. And you know what, they're not your enemies. Your loved ones are there to console you. No, they're not going to understand what you're going through unless they have lost a child themselves. The worst part of losing a child was when a person would come up to me and say, "Hey, I know how you feel." "Are you

SERIOUS?" I would yell out. "Unless you've lost a child or had a miscarriage, you would never know how I feel. Never!" Could I have handled it in a different way when that person made that statement? Yes, I could have. But do you think in that time your mind is saying, 'be nice. Understand where they're coming from.' No. Honestly, your mind is saying get the heck up out my face. Just being Honest.

One thing you must do is let it out. Go in the bathroom, bedroom, wherever you need to, and scream, cry, shout it all out. Holding in your feelings is not going to help you through this time at all. You may cry all day. At the beginning, that's OK; you have just lost your child. You are filled with a tremendous amount of emotions. Your hormones are running all over the place. When my son passed, I cried daily sometimes. Just drove out in the country by myself, parked my car and screamed, hitting my steering wheel and windows. Sometimes I sat for hours. Then, I would pull myself back together and ride back to my parents' home. Was it healthy? No. Did it help me get my anger out? Yes. I didn't harm anyone, and I

didn't harm myself. I might have bruises, but I didn't hurt myself. I think the bulk of my anger was towards GOD. I was so upset at him. I would yell out the most hateful things. I couldn't understand what I had done to make him take my child. I wasn't praying and going to church as I should; but to take my son. I was totally reflecting on the wrong person. Yes, I was angry also at the person who took my son's life. Honestly, I wanted to take his life the way he took my son's. I knew I couldn't do it; but I really wanted to.

During my miscarriages, anger was a stage for me each time. I would see women walking around smoking and pregnant, and still having healthy babies. Then I have a miscarriage and had never touched a cigarette during my pregnancy. "How do you let them keep their babies and me not?" I talked to God daily, blaming him. This went on for weeks. Anger begins your process of healing; usually no one skips this stage.

Let's look at other ways to let your anger out. Walking is a good one. Just getting some fresh air and letting your mind be free, not being cooped up in a house can do wonders. Reading, drawing, or joining small groups for loss also help. I became such a reader after this time. I read a lot of my books, books on faith, encouragement, and grief. These books probably would have helped me understand what I was going through if I had been experiencing it at the very moment; but this all started after I went through all the stages. It was then that I started reading more books and understanding what I was going through and why. On the next couple lines write down some things that calm you and helps you to relax.

I feel relaxed when I

_____
_____
_____
_____
_____
_____
_____
_____
_____
_____
_____
_____
_____
_____
_____
_____
_____
_____
_____
_____
_____
_____
_____
_____

_____
_____
_____
_____
_____
_____
_____
_____
_____
_____
_____
_____
_____
_____
_____
_____
_____
_____
_____
_____
_____
_____
_____
_____
_____

Bargaining

"The bargaining stage is an attempt to negotiate with someone who seemingly has control over the life-and-death situation.".

Bargaining. Did you ever say, "God, if you bring him back now, I will change my life"? Or, "just take me. Bring him back and take me." Or, "let me just play this day back over. I would change how I treated people." Or how about, "I will spend more time with them, like I should have." I truly believe that bargaining is something everyone does. I told myself I didn't do that, but I did. I didn't really have a relationship with God at that time; but I still was bargaining. I knew he had something to do with my child being gone, so I was going to bargain anyway I could. Basically, bargaining is making a secret deal with God to bring back your loved one. That's it in a nutshell. I remember thinking I could make a deal with the Devil. I would have done anything. This was a shorter phase for me. In bargaining, you quickly understand this just won't happen. For the most part,

you're bargaining with something you
have no control over. Nothing you can say
can reverse what has happened."

What did you do to try to bargain?

_____
_____
_____
_____
_____
_____
_____
_____
_____
_____
_____
_____
_____
_____
_____
_____
_____
_____
_____
_____
_____
_____

_____
_____
_____
_____
_____
_____
_____
_____
_____
_____
_____
_____
_____
_____
_____
_____
_____
_____
_____
_____
_____
_____
_____
_____
_____
_____

Sonya Johnson

Believing in something is having hope.
Hope of something to happen. When is it
going to happen, I prayed, I fasted, and I
sustained? Nothing, Nothing.

Depression

There are two types of depression that are associated with mourning. The first one is a reaction to practical implications relating to the loss. Sadness and regret predominate this type of depression. We worry about the costs and burial. We worry that, in our grief, we have spent less time with others that depend on us. This phase may be eased by simple clarification and reassurance. We may need a bit of helpful cooperation and a few kind words.

APA Reference Axelrod, J. (2018). The 5 Stages of Grief & Loss. Psych Central. Retrieved on October 30, 2018, from https://psychcentral.com/lib/the-5-stages-of-loss-and-grief/

Depression happens to almost all of us, whether we want to admit it or not; it does. And it comes in different forms. Depression can make or break you. You know, I get very amused when people say, 'oh, you don't need to speak to a therapist about your problems. You don't need to do that; that's only for crazy people. No one, and I mean no one, should tell you who you should or should not speak to

when it comes to depression. A lot of people have lost their lives, because they didn't reach out and speak to someone for various reasons. Maybe it was forbidden in their family, or they thought that people would talk about them. Maybe they just didn't feel comfortable at all. I'm telling you that you will need an outlet. You will need to talk to someone; whether it's a doctor, a friend, or God. You must talk to someone. If you get to the point where you're secluding yourself, or isolating yourself, then you need to go and see a professional.

Through my bouts of depression, I did eventually speak to a pastor; but first I went to the doctor. I did get on medication because I myself felt suicidal. I realized I was abusing cigarettes and alcohol to soothe my pain. I did it late at night. I would put my son to bed, sneak outside, look up at the sky, and cry. No one knew what I was going through. I hid it so well. I would get up, go to work, have a normal day. People would say how I was doing very well, and they were happy to see me out and about. But that was all a front. I knew how to cover up very well. I

would eat small amounts in front of people, but at home I didn't eat. When I made dinner for my son, I would put a small spoon full on my plate, just to make him feel I was eating with him. He was five at the time, so he didn't notice how much I ate. When I noticed the change in me, I eventually went and got properly diagnosed. I was diagnosed with Depression and PTSD; Post-Traumatic Stress Disorder.

PTSD is a mental condition, that results in a series of emotional and physical reactions in individuals who have either witnessed or experienced a traumatic event. These events can cause you to fear for your personal life and wellbeing. Examples include car accidents, sexual and physical assault, abuse, or in my case, the death of my son at the hands of my then fiancé. I was started on a medication and took it faithfully for about two months. After that, I started to realize, I hadn't cried almost the entire time I had been taking it. This was good in a way. I realized I didn't have any emotions whatsoever. When I smiled, it didn't feel genuine.

Sonya Johnson

When I thought about my son that had passed, it was like I had no feelings. I didn't like that at all. I knew it was good to have a good cry here and there. I felt like I was a walking zombie, just getting through the day. I slowly stopped taking the pills and concentrated on my faith. By this time, I was introduced to GOD and learning his word.

Everyone has their different beliefs, and I can't tell you how to heal. I can only give my experiences.

I went back to depression shortly after my miscarriage. This was over seven years after the death of my son. By this time, I had given birth to another baby. Having that miscarriage took me back to when I lost my son. I went into the same depression. All those wounds opened again. Even though I had given birth after him, the emotions came back with this new loss. The feelings ate at me for weeks. I knew my husband was hurting too; but I felt as if he wasn't hurting the same as me. This was his first time losing a child, but I couldn't talk to him. I began to isolate him. This went on for weeks. It wasn't until one day I was at work, and

my friend asked me, "How is your husband taking it." It was then I realized, he had lost a child too. I wasn't alone and if I could talk to anyone about OUR loss, it should be him. I immediately texted him, expressing my feelings and the need for us to talk when we got off work. He agreed. After we talked, I came to learn he was grieving just as I was. That moment of just us talking and expressing how we felt, opened a new line of communication, and took both of us out of our depression.

"What is this I am feeling? Loneliness, heartache, numbness just to name a few. I sink into a hole. A hole so deep, I only see a flash of light when I look up. It's cold, dark and lonely. I feel like I only have myself. I don't want to bother people with my problems or feelings. They will say I need help; I am losing it. But, am I crazy? Can I live knowing that my child won't be living life on earth with me? Can I make it through the day without those thoughts of suicide? If I take my life now, I will see my baby. Or will I? Do you go to heaven when you take your life, or hell? Does anyone know the answer? But wait, I have my other son

that is here, alive, and well. What will happen to him if I take my life? Who will care for him? Will he ever understand that I had to go be with his brother? THEN it hits me! NO, I HAVE TO GET THROUGH THIS AND LIVE FOR MY SON. HE HAS TO KNOW I WILL NOT LEAVE HIM, AND WE CAN HEAL THROUGH THIS TOGETHER."

A Mother's Pain, Heaven's Gain

Depression_____
_____
_____
_____
_____
_____
_____
_____
_____
_____
_____
_____
_____
_____
_____
_____
_____
_____
_____
_____
_____
_____
_____
_____
_____
_____
_____
_____

Sonya Johnson

_____
_____
_____
_____
_____
_____
_____
_____
_____
_____
_____
_____
_____
_____
_____
_____
_____
_____
_____
_____
_____
_____
_____
_____
_____

Acceptance

Accepting that your loved one is physically gone is the last stage. Recognizing this is your permanent reality is just that. You know now that you will never see your child again till you leave this earth. I used to fear death when I was younger. I would always think, 'where would I go?' (before I was born again Christian). How would my family live without me? I was so concerned about my parents. Since after my son passed, my belief in GOD has kept me going. I no longer fear death. Not saying I want to go tomorrow; but I smile when I think about when it's my time to go. I always imagine me opening my eyes and walking up that pearly white road, my son standing down a couple feet in front of me with his arms open. I know when it's my time, I will be ready.

Chapter 4

Where do I go from here?

It has been nineteen years since my son passed, and somedays it feels like it was only yesterday. I still think about him all the time, especially when holidays come around. I think about him the most on his birthday. I imagine how he would look now, how tall he would be, if he would get along with his siblings. The first couple years, I had trouble every holiday; but as the years went on, it got better. IT WILL get easier. Everyone grieves at their own pace; but we all grieve.

A friend of my son's passed not too long ago, and their mother told me that someone told her it will NOT get easier. I informed her that what she had heard was totally not true. Now for the first couple years, you might feel as if this gets harder and harder to deal with. And if you do feel this way, it's NORMAL. This might be the time when you seek comfort in talking to other women who have been through it, a therapist, God, or maybe your personal physician. IT DOES get

easier, but not by doing it on your own. Whether it be with spiritual help or pharmaceutical, you can get through it.

Although you will never, ever forget your child, the grieving will get easier. You will eventually be able to enjoy holidays, get through their birthdays easier, and talk about it. The key is, when you are able to talk about it without crying; you're healing.

To heal is the monumental breaking point. It takes years to heal. Healing is a process. That process is slow and steady. You may have setbacks. Some things may trigger you. For me, seeing other children on the news that have been murdered by a parent or co-parent, triggers me. I sit down and pray for the family. Then it brings me back to my son. I must take a moment to just sit and reflect on the good times I had with him, and how I have helped others get through their grief process.

Take time for yourself. Get out as much as possible. Find a good church home. PRAY. Support groups are very good. You get to hear other women and sometimes men, share stories of their

loss. Talking is the most healing thing you can do for yourself. DO NOT keep your feelings bottled up. That does more harm than good.

When my time ends on this earth, I know without a doubt I will be greeted by my son in the gates of heaven. I imagine him standing with his arms open and saying. "Mommy I've missed you so much......"

Prayer: Lord, keep me uplifted when I appear to be weak or down. When I think of my child, let me think of the good times and precious moments I had with him.

A Mother's Pain, Heaven's Gain

My conversation when I see you
again_____
_____
_____
_____
_____
_____
_____
_____
_____
_____
_____
_____
_____
_____
_____
_____
_____
_____
_____
_____
_____
_____
_____
_____
_____
_____
_____
_____
_____

Sonya Johnson

Poems

I Found Peace

I have started to find peace in knowing you're not with me. I cried and cried to no end. It has been hard to think that I will never see you again on earth. But knowing you're in heaven makes it a little easier of course. I can see you in the heavens with your great grandmother and great grandfather, them telling you stories of how I was as a child, and making you laugh aloud. Tears come but quickly go away, when I think of the joy that you brought my way. Although I will miss you in every way, I have finally found peace to be able to make it through those hard days.

Sonya Johnson

I Never Seen You Before

When I found out the test was positive, my heart skipped a beat. I was pregnant, OMG! I planned and counted down the days until you should arrive. I even went out and bought a couple of supplies. It was almost two months when we informed everyone in the family. The joy and happiness was overwhelming.

Then one morning I woke up in pain. I looked down and there was a red stain. The fear and panic I felt was real. Something was wrong. "Oh no, I can't deal." When the doctor told me, you were gone, a piece of me left right along. I think of you from time to time. Were you a girl or boy? I wish I could have known. I believe there will come a time, when God will let me know.

_____
_____
_____
_____
_____
_____
_____
_____

_____

_____

_____

_____

_____

_____

_____

_____

_____

_____

_____

_____

_____

_____

_____

_____

_____

_____

_____

_____

_____

_____

_____

_____

_____

Made in the USA
Monee, IL
22 November 2021

82387223R00066

A Mother's Pain, Heaven's Gain
A guidebook for dealing with the loss
of a child
By Sonya Johnson
Copyright 2020 by Sonya Johnson
All Rights Reserved
ISBN:9781671754584

A
MOTHER'S PAIN,
HEAVEN'S GAIN

A guidebook for dealing with the loss of a
child

By Sonya Johnson

watch me ascend toward Darkhaven's newest witchy resident.

When I reach Sofía, she sucks in a sharp breath. Her lungs spasm at the abrupt rush of air. I hear them clench, shrinking and widening, desperate to feed her body the necessary oxygen it requires to stay alive. If her lungs could think, if they could foresee my plans for her, would they give up now? Would they save her the despair of future agony by ceasing effort, taking her life this very second?

I stop in front of her, smiling, waiting. She has stopped breathing. Her lungs struggle to feed her organs, using only what is trapped inside them. I think I can hear their plea, their scream for a fresh supply of air, but she must not hear it. She does not release the breath she is holding. I imagine she is waiting for me to break first, but that will never happen. Not because I am overly cruel but because I am strangely curious to know if Sofía can hold her breath so long she passes out.

Her lungs clench tighter, making a soft, squeaky sound that echoes around us. The others must hear it because there is ruffling behind me. The hunters are stepping forward, and I know they have every intention of intervening. Still, I won't break first. I will *never* break first.

Malik is at my side. I see him from the corner of my vision, but I never break eye contact with Sofía. Only when she falters, expelling the used, useless breath from her lungs, do I look away. She stumbles backward so quickly, she falls.

My leader catches her, and he gives me a piercing glare. Malik's narrowed eyes pinch his features, making him appear far more dangerous than I know him to be. His hardened gaze threatens my very existence, but I know he will never follow through with the silent turmoil between us.

I turn on my heels and skip toward the manor, softly

giggling while the night hums all around me.

I swipe the steam from the mirror and stare at my reflection. My hair hangs raggedly at my shoulders, a sopping wet mess after my shower. I run my fingers through my tresses, smoothing tangles as I go. I continue to hum a tune heard only in my head when the distinct sound of my bedroom door opening distracts me. Quickly, I dress and exit my bathroom, stopping short of crossing the threshold into my room.

Sofía is there, standing in the doorway, not fully committing to entering my personal space but not leaving either.

"Hello, Sofía," I say.

She does not respond, so I walk closer, halting only when she is directly before me, close enough where I can reach out and grab on to her flesh and bone.

Her breath hitches, so I know she is afraid, but she maintains eye contact. Her eyes are the color of milk chocolate, smooth and dark, with specks of golden bronze scattered around her pupil. I imagine my own, neon crimson and swirling with magic. I wonder if this intimidates her. Now that she knows I am not simply a vampire, what does she see when she looks at me? A fallen witch? An enemy?

"Holland told me you're different," she begins.

"So you came to tell me what I already know?" I ask, both intrigued and annoyed by her persistence and courage.

"You're a vampire who can access magic," she says softly. Her voice is low, her words coated by her disbelief. When she speaks, she does not ask questions. She simply states her words—again, reminding me of something I already know to be true.

"Ah," I say, understanding her true intentions. "You want to see? You want a show? You want me to use magic to validate what you *think* you saw earlier tonight."

Sofía swallows hard, and I quiver at the sound. Her esophagus constricts, spilling her spit into the empty pit at her core. I feel my own stomach churn from hunger. My gaze flickers to Sofía's neck, and she sucks in a loud breath. She wavers, becoming unsteady on her feet.

"You're not like the others," she whispers.

Her words ground me, rooting me in place. Meeting her eyes, I blink away my desire to feed.

"What others?" I ask. "The vampires of this nest?"

"Um...yeah," she says. Her hands are balled into fists at her sides, and her arms are shaking from strain. Even this fascinates me. Everything she does, from the way her fear affects her body to the way she sounds when she moves, it all excites me, interests me—almost as if she is the first mortal I have ever seen in performance.

"Correct," I confirm. "You're right. I am not like them."

"So *what* are you?" she asks, repeating her question from earlier. She sounds different this time. Earlier, her disbelief was evident in her tone. Now, curiosity overpowers her fear, and her eagerness is reflected in her voice.

"Strong," I say simply.

I chuckle. I enjoy the way my confession processes in her mind. It bleeds into her features, from realization to shock to terror, and each emotion amuses me.

"They have no idea, do they?" Sofía asks, her voice a harsh whisper. I don't like the way it targets me, lashing out as if it intends to harm.

Still, her question catches me off guard, so I think about it for a moment, letting the silence linger. I scan her frame, soft but muscular, looking for any clues that may help me understand her intentions. She gives away nothing, and this frustrates me more than her candor.

"About what?" I ask finally. "What don't they know?"

"They have no idea how evil you actually are," she says plainly, no longer questioning her beliefs. She states her hypothesis with firmness. The positivity there only irritates me further.

But I smile, finding that even though she disappoints me every time she opens her mouth, I am quite enjoying my time with Sofía. Ever since she arrived, I have had so many questions, and her answers have left a lot to be desired. Perhaps now we will get somewhere.

"I think you're getting ahead of yourself, Sofía," I say. "You speak as though you may turn them against me at a moment's notice. But if you were them, what would you deem more important? That they may not be privy to my capabilities, or that they are utterly unaware of the magic you have been using against them since you arrived?"

She doesn't respond, but her silence speaks volumes.

"You have been using magic to subtly influence the others, manipulating their emotions," I say. She stiffens in an attempt to argue with me, but I hold out my hand, silencing her. "I don't need you to confirm what I already know."

"But I haven't—"

"*Sofía*," I say. I *tsk* her, waving my index finger back and forth. My tongue smacks against the roof of my mouth, and the sound surrounds us.

"You could never prove it," she says, grinding her teeth.

"I don't need to prove it," I say plainly. "Who do you think they will believe? You or me? A stranger or their friend? Once the accusation has been made, the damage is done."

"They said you're not acting right, Ava," Sofía says. She breaks eye contact to glance down at the amulet that hangs from my neck. "It's that *thing*, isn't it? It's influencing you, turning you evil. Holland told me about the amulet, about what you . . . *protect*." She uses air quotes to emphasize her point.

Angered that she would dare to even glance at my power source, I reach forward, forcing Sofía's head upright so that her eyes meet mine again. I keep my hand wrapped around her throat, but I fight the urge to squeeze so hard I break bones. Still, her eyes betray her fear. She reaches for my hand, scratching at my skin, but I do not relent. Instead, I step closer until our noses nearly touch.

"Don't test me, Sofía," I hiss. "You will *never* best me."

"Ava?"

Holland's shaky voice spills from the hallway. I glance at him as he steps closer, reaching an arm for Sofía as if to offer *her* comfort.

"Let her go," he says. He speaks softly, never raising his voice, never ordering me what to do. He offers merely a suggestion, and I decide to appease him, releasing Sofía from my grasp and taking a single step backward.

Sofía takes in a quick breath, hacking dramatically and falling against the doorframe. I roll my eyes even as Holland reaches for the witch. She leans against him, but he keeps his eyes on me.

"You know what I find interesting?" I ask. "The vampire who supposedly killed your coven is gone, yet you remain. Why? Why stay?"

"Seriously, Ava?" Holland asks. "What's wrong with you?"

I ignore him, keeping my focus on the witch who appears to have overcome her recent duress rather quickly. Sofía stands tall beside Holland, as if my simple suggestion that she may be lying offends her. I can't possibly be the only one in this house who believes she has ulterior motives.

"I assume you'll be leaving tomorrow," I say. "After all, you came to kill a vampire. Plenty are dead."

"But maybe not the right ones," she says, seething.

I narrow my eyes at her, my anger washing over me. The amulet buzzes to life, catching the attention of both witches before me. Holland's gaze doesn't stray from the black onyx crystal, but Sofía's does. She averts her vision back to me, challenging the monster she has awakened.

"Careful, girl," I say. "Mercy is only granted by the weak."

There is something different about the trees. They sway from side to side, leaves fluttering loudly, branches straining to remain erect by an invisible force, yet there is no wind. Clouds loom overhead, stagnant and true, an ominous threat of what is to come. The warning gleam of a storm on the horizon coats the air, the smell of incoming rain strong and heavy. The air is thick with promise, making it hard to breathe, to blink.

I don't recall it being this foggy. The memory of that fateful night is burned into my mind, but tonight, it is changing, transforming into something menacing and foreboding.

The mist intensifies tenfold. I struggle to breathe, sucking in quick breaths that linger against the back of my throat even after I am desperate to expel them. I choke, my lungs burning from contact with the air, wet and musty.

Despite the harsh changes, I recognize this place. Even as I slumber, safe within the confines of the manor, I am aware that I am dreaming, that I am not truly here—at least, not physically. My mind is alive, my imagination rapid-firing the details of that night that played out so many moons ago.

I watch them from a distance as the sun begins to set, casting shadows, distorting features, turning my once-heroes into villains. I watch myself—a young girl on the verge of a brutal attack. She has no idea her life is soon to change.

I am small and feeble, with a fire burning deep in my soul, a red-hot fury sparked by the desire to appease my elders. I never knew my devotion would be so hard to shake. That girl has no idea it will take countless betrayals and a tsunami of bloodshed to sever her link to the witches.

I don't know why I am here, why my mind keeps forcing me to relive this particular moment. The night my father was murdered by rogue vampires is seared into my spirit energy, the pain never lessening even though I am no longer that fragile little girl. Still, guilt hovers overhead, overshadowing the darkening sky. It wraps around me, edging me closer to my past and away from the sanctuary of the forest.

I have relived this past memory countless times, and I know every second of every moment. I know exactly how it plays out. Even when I am not in this place, I can still hear my father's screams, my mother's wails. I still feel my uncertainty. I may not have witnessed my father's death, but that little girl was aware of it, of what happened.

I ask myself again, *Why am I here?* I still have no answer. My mind may be alive, but my lips are mute. The spirits have no intention of guiding me through this vision, so I must see myself through it.

I think about this place, about everything that happened that night. I watch my family, their movements repetitive in my mind, but something is off. I notice the differences, all the little ways that girl no longer resembles the woman I have become. When she smiles, there is a glint in her eyes, a glisten I lost long ago. I can thank my mother for that, for the loss of life that once made me vibrant and happy.

My parents are beside her. They are content as they celebrate life, enjoying what they assume is just one of many more days they have together. They are wrong. Tonight, their lives will be upended courtesy of a single careless mistake. The simple decision to picnic in the forest, venturing deep in the woods, creates a cataclysmic event with long-lasting ripple effects.

I take another step forward, and I am greeted by the tree line. One more step and I will be in the field, where wildflowers are overgrown just enough to hide the blanket and basket.

The wind is shifting now. The clouds roll in, covering the setting sun. The world darkens, and I have to squint to focus on them. I take another step, but they don't see me. Burdened by the desire to escape, they never even notice how close I have come. But even if they looked up at this exact moment, meeting my gaze, would they see me? This is but a memory.

Quickly, my parents abandon this place, carrying the childlike version of myself toward safety yet finding only danger. I don't have to follow to know what happens next.

Mother leaves. Father fights the vampires. I never see him again.

I don't follow them. Instead, I stare at the space where they sat only moments ago, sensing the rush of residual heat in the spots where their bodies rested against the cool, hard earth. It dissipates quickly, unlike this dream.

The amulet at my clavicle electrifies, stinging my skin, urging me forward. So I follow, like I always do. I stomp through the mud, tearing through the overgrown brush along the forest floor.

I reach them easily, and just as I thought, they have no idea I am here. Mother is screaming, and Father is ushering her away. The little girl is crying in her mother's arms. I meet her eyes, cloudy and muddled by tears, and she blinks them away, never breaking eye contact with me.

I take a deep breath and hold it, convincing myself she can actually see me because this part is new. This is something that has never happened, not in all the years I have visited this place, reliving this moment.

The girl points at the path our father just disappeared down, and I follow the trail with my gaze. I expel my breath as my lungs spasm, desperate for oxygen, and I nod at the forest, understanding her unspoken request. I never look back at the girl, but I feel her eyes on me, and I sense her satisfaction as I obey her order.

When I reach him, I grab on to the crystal, wrapping my fingers around the black onyx stone. I am harnessing its power, commanding the entity trapped within to save my father, and it does. Eagerly, it obeys me as easily as I obeyed the girl. The rogue vampires surrounding my father combust, exploding into ash, caking the ground in gray.

My father turns to face me. From his sharp jawline, dusted with salt-and-pepper hair, to his stark black tousled locks to his lengthy, defined frame, everything about him feels familiar, as though I saw him only yesterday. He even smells the same, like sage and mint, just like I remember.

His clothing is torn and charred from his fire magic, and blood stains his neck where the rogues were feeding only moments ago. I cringe as my gaze lingers there, where his wound slowly heals.

I tell him I saved him, and he smiles. I speak, and though my lips never move, my voice echoes around us, swirling and tightening, coiling like a snake. It grips us tighter, my words turning dark—no longer a promise, now a threat.

As my father approaches me, my dream shifts yet again. He morphs as he walks closer, his features blurring until the man before me is no longer the person I remember from my past. The face of a stranger stares back at me. Even though I have seen this person many times, always haunting my dreams, I still don't know his true identity. He remains an outsider, an intruder in my mind.

"Ava, you must destroy the amulet," he says, never straying from his script.

In every dream, he reminds me of this, over and over again, like he is merely a recorded presence, a voice on tape rather than flesh and bone. I have memorized every word he speaks.

I shake my head, squeezing the black onyx crystal tighter in my palm, using it against him. I want this man to leave, and I want my father to return.

"You don't understand," he warns, his gaze fluttering to the crystal in my hand. "That thing is like a homing beacon, and creatures all around the world can sense its power. The longer it is in existence, the greater danger you are in. You must get rid of it."

I open my eyes and stare at the ceiling. The fan overhead swooshes calmingly, a soft breeze settling over my bare skin. The bedsheets are tangled at my feet, wrapped tightly around my legs.

I sit upright and lean against the headboard. I am alone in my bedroom. I frown as I glance at the bedside clock, noting the sun set hours ago. It is rare for me to sleep in later than Jasik and even rarer not to be woken by the sounds of the manor coming alive.

I dangle my legs over the side of the bed, body stiff from too much sleep. I crane my neck from side to side and roll my shoulders, hoping to ease the tension. It doesn't. Everything in my body feels tight and rigid—even my brain feels stiff, like it is crammed into my skull. My headache intensifies with each passing second.

I pull back the thick drapes that cover my bedroom window and stare into the distance. Darkhaven is cloaked in darkness, but the moon shines brightly overhead. Stars cast an eerie glow over the forest that surrounds the manor. There are no signs of the other vampires, but I assume they linger, slurping down breakfast or patrolling the woods.

Quickly I complete my morning routine, washing and dressing, and I am exiting my bedroom twenty minutes later. I close the door tightly behind me and turn to head downstairs, nearly colliding with Hikari. She narrows her eyes at me, her gaze scanning the length of my short frame. Her silence is unsettling.

"Ava," she says by way of greeting. Her pixie locks are spiky and shiny, gleaming in the hallway's low light. I can smell the subtle scent of blood on her breath, and it makes my stomach grumble.

"Hikari," I reply, confused by her reaction to our encounter but too hungry to question it.

I slide past her and make my way toward the stairs. When I turn to descend, I glance back. She is still standing by my bedroom door, watching as I retreat.

When I reach the bottom landing, I spot Jeremiah and Holland. They are relaxing in the sitting room, a book in Holland's hand and a mug of blood in Jeremiah's. They both glance up as I turn to enter the dining room. No one speaks, but I wave anyway.

In the kitchen, Malik is enjoying breakfast. He stops drinking, holding his mug midair, and watches me carefully. Suddenly acutely aware of my surroundings, I roll my eyes, grumbling internally as I grab a mug and empty the contents of a blood bag into it. I stare at the microwave, waiting as the seconds tick on.

"How are you feeling today, Ava?" Malik asks.

"I'm *fine*," I say pointedly.

I don't hide my annoyance. Just about every day now, I am asked how I feel, and the constant prodding is frustrating, to say the least. I would feel a lot better if they just left me alone.

"I see," he says slowly, emphasizing both words.

Anger is bubbling in my gut, threatening to spill over.

I spin on my heels, facing him. He remains seated but sets down his mug and leans back in his chair, crossing his arms over his chest as he waits for my response. Silently, he dares me to confront him, as though he expected this reaction.

"Just say it," I groan. Malik may be emotionally unreadable, but when something needs to be said, there is no other vampire in this house who makes it as obvious as he does. Something is on his mind, and he is itching to reveal it.

"Say what?" he asks, arching a brow, pretending like there isn't an unspoken argument brewing between us.

"Whatever you're holding back," I say. "Get it off your chest."

"I'm concerned," he says plainly.

"About?" I ask, frustration growing. If he's the one who wants to talk, why do I feel like I am forcing him to speak?

Malik glances at the black onyx crystal, and I feel the stone heat against my skin. It sizzles on contact, but I am certain Malik hasn't noticed the change. Still, the stone reacts, understanding Malik to be a threat to its existence. It only calms when his gaze settles on mine again.

"I'm fine," I repeat.

"You're not," he argues. "And the fact that you continue trying to convince us that you are only concerns me more."

I huff sharply, expelling the breath from my lungs until they spasm. I enjoy the pain. It's better than talking about my feelings with Malik.

"I don't know what you want me to say, Malik. I *am* fine."

"Ava, that stone is influencing you. Little by little, day by day, we see less of you and more of . . . *it*."

"It?" I ask, even though I understand his meaning.

"The entity," he says firmly. "The stone is losing its control over it, and whatever the witches created is seeping into you. I'm afraid you aren't strong enough to fight it."

"That's funny," I say. "The last time I checked, I'm the only hybrid in this nest. I think that makes me pretty damn powerful, Malik."

I don't hide my annoyance, and the threat of my tone lingers. At this, Malik stands abruptly, closing the space between us. I stand tall even though he towers over me, but I refuse to show weakness.

"Ava, we *know* something is amiss," Malik says. "You have been acting strangely ever since you took control of that amulet. The longer you deny it, the more difficult it will be to save you."

"And let me guess . . . When it comes down to saving them or me, you'll choose them," I say. "I've heard this threat before, Malik."

"I don't want to hurt you, Ava."

"But you will if you have to," I say.

He nods, never speaking the words aloud. I suppose I don't need him to. I'm used to being the sacrifice.

"I understand," I say. "If there is one thing we both agree on, it's protecting what matters when we feel threatened."

Malik frowns, furrowing his brows, and briefly, I worry he won't understand my veiled threat.

I step forward and angle my head back so he can see me fully, so he can understand I am not threatened by him. Malik and I are standing so close we share the same air, the same breath. He remains unyielding, eyes hard, while I chuckle, the sound rumbling from my chest.

"I *will* destroy that amulet, Ava."

"Not if it destroys you first," I whisper.

Malik takes several steps back, never averting his gaze. His hands are balled into fists at his sides. His muscles strain, jaw clenched, and I can practically taste the anger radiating from him. It tastes like seared flesh. I lick my lips.

"Do you see now?" he says. "Do you see how it is influencing her?"

I frown, but before I can respond, the door to the butler's pantry flings open, and Jasik strides into the kitchen. He is tall, like his brother, and leanly built. His jacket is covered in soot, and he smells like ash. I scrunch my nose at the scent wafting closer.

"You may have fooled your sire, Ava, but you do not fool me," Malik says. "He believes you still mourn the witches and that the death of your mother is the reason for your actions. I know better."

"She just needs time," Jasik says.

"We cannot risk our lives," Malik hisses, his frustration getting the best of him. "It's not safe here, not when the amulet is under her protection."

"I can help her," Jasik argues.

"There isn't time," Malik says. "It is becoming too powerful. We must destroy it before it becomes too great even for us."

"Ava," Jasik says, ignoring his brother and stepping closer. He holds out his hand, offering it to me. "Come with me. I have something I want to show you."

My gaze flutters between the two vampires and the offering before me, and I opt for the easiest exit, taking Jasik's hand. When his palm glides against mine, the world seems to silence. The rapid beats of Malik's heart no longer echo in my mind. The buzzing at my clavicle no longer burns against my skin. Instead, all I feel is a tingling sensation in my palm and the heat pulsating from Jasik's body as I close the space between us.

"I have something for you," he whispers, tucking loose strands of hair behind my ear. "It's outside."

In the backyard, he leads me away from the manor and closer to the cemetery. His grip on my hand tightens as I suck in a loud breath. I try not to think about the souls gone and the bodies buried. I try not to think about the days that have passed since I last visited them.

As we approach, I notice something new. A headstone directly beside Will's. Carved from the same stone that memorializes those we lost that night, the tombstone is etched with my mother's name: *Tatiana López*.

A sleek box is nestled on the ground in front of the stone. I withdraw from Jasik's grasp and kneel before it, letting my body sink into the earth. I hold my breath as I run my hand over the familiar box, the wood cool to the touch. Jasik crouches beside me, hand resting on my back. He rubs softly as he speaks.

"I gathered your mother's ashes, and I placed them in this box," he says.

"We used to keep stones in it," I whisper. "After charging them under the full moon, we would place them in this for safekeeping."

"It was outside. I think . . . " He pauses before adding, "I think that's why it wasn't destroyed."

I nod, sniffling as I grab on to it. It is surprisingly light, even though it houses her cremains. I cradle it to my chest, gripping the wood tightly. My mother was a powerful, formidable witch. Under her roof, I spent so many years fearful—afraid to disappoint her, afraid to upset her, afraid she wouldn't accept me, afraid I would never see her again. Now, I fear for her soul. Where is she? Did her misdeeds overshadow all the good she did? Will she spend an eternity paying for those mistakes?

"I know how much it hurts to lose your family, Ava," Jasik says. "And I know this doesn't make up for everything that happened, but I do hope it will help lessen the pain—maybe ease the burden."

I glance up at my sire, vision blurred by my tears. Jasik smiles at me, but it never reaches his eyes. Those two swirling, crimson pools stare back at me, and within them, I see his fear.

TWO

I think about my nestmates as I trek through the forest, intent on patrolling the woods. After Jasik's heartfelt gesture, I needed space. He may believe in me, but the others certainly don't. The stench of fear drove me away, and as I hike through the brush, I have little desire to return.

The farther I am from the manor—and our annoying new houseguest—the better I feel. The tension in my head eases, and the world becomes clearer. But the better I feel physically, the worse I feel emotionally. I can't stop thinking about my nightmares, about the mysterious man who keeps warning me about the amulet's dark power, and about the witch who refuses to leave Darkhaven. True coincidences rarely occur in Darkhaven, yet I am drowning in them now.

As the sole caretaker of the evil entity created by the witches, I am burdened by this amulet. Without Will, I can trust no one else to be powerful enough to withstand its power. That means it's up to me to keep it safe.

Then Sofía magically showed up with every intention of killing the very rogue vampire I was hunting. The chances of that are too slim to ignore, yet that's all the hunters seem to do. *Ignore her.* As I was leaving the manor to patrol, I heard her laugh, hearty and loud, and as I closed the front door, desperate to avoid an awkward encounter, Holland joined her by laughing as well. I don't know what bothers me more: the fact that Sofía was unruffled by my threat or the fact that she's turning all my friends against me.

The rogue vampire she sought is dead, so why is she still around? Better yet, why am I the only one who thinks something is off about her? This whole situation is strange. Witches settled in Darkhaven long ago, and we rarely see new faces in town. Darkhaven may be an idyllic place to live, but we do a great job of staying off the radar. Tourists rarely find us, so how did she? Sofía claims to be born from longtime family friends, but I'm not sure I believe that. *Mamá* would have told me about her.

I think about that rogue vampire and the last words he said to me. He made a promise to *him*—whoever *he* is. I stop short, letting his confession wash over me. The rogue vampire was taking orders from someone else, someone who made it clear I wasn't to be harmed. I'm not sure who this mysterious man is or why he needs me alive, but what are the chances it is unrelated to my mysterious dreamwalker? Could it be that the rogue vampire and I were being visited by the same man?

I grasp the amulet, running my thumb over the jagged stone. I need to learn more about this crystal, about the entity inside, and about the man who fears it so much.

I kick at the ground with my feet, sending a scattering of brush showering before me. How am I supposed to research anything without consulting Holland? When he arrived, he brought a library of occult books with him. As far as I know, those books, paired with the ones already at the manor, make up the largest collection in this area. I have little chance of researching this unnoticed. I know I promised to be honest with the vampires, but with Sofía happily digging her claws into the flesh of my comrades, I'm not quite ready to share. I don't trust her, but they do. Sadly, this means only one thing: I can't trust my friends either.

When I reach the edge of the forest, I take a single step past the tree line, letting the devastation sink in. It's strange to think that I was raised here, because it's nothing but rubble now. Charred wood planks are piled in a heap. The grass surrounding the house was scorched and is now black and dead. Bits of broken, burned furniture have been tossed aside. Shattered glass is scattered across the lawn. I can picture the firefighters drenching the flames, extinguishing the fire, leaving behind nothing but a sloppy mess. I spent my entire life within these walls, but it barely resembles a house now.

The bright-yellow do-not-cross tape surrounds what remains. Much of the house's frame is still erect, the studs swaying slightly in the breeze, ready to fall at a moment's notice. They'll topple over, joining the dark abyss that consists of my former basement. I squint, staring at the pit, still keeping my distance, ever fearful that passersby will spot me. I remain in the darkness, letting memories of my time here loop in my mind. The film reel is sad and short because so little of my childhood was happy.

I sigh heavily as I step under the caution tape, ensuring it remains undisturbed as I walk closer to the destruction. In all the years of practicing magic in this house, I'm shocked this didn't happen sooner—but for less ominous reasons. When I was younger, I was reckless with my magic, staying up late to practice elemental control. Once, my bedsheets caught fire.

Another time, I flooded the top floor, causing a waterfall to seep through the floorboards and stain the downstairs ceiling a murky gray color. With the house gone, the truth of those moments will reside only in my memory now.

I walk slowly, my weight crunching broken glass beneath my boots. The night air is warmer tonight, the promise of spring on the horizon. Spring is a time of rebirth, of renewal. I wonder if the change of seasons will be good for me. Maybe this year will be kinder than the last. I suppose it has to be. After all, I did die last year.

As I loop around the house, lost in my thoughts, I bypass debris, sidestepping mounds of memories from a past life. When I am nearly at the front of the house, I come to an abrupt halt. A figure is crouched by the opening that was once my front door. The barrier is gone now, so I can see her clearly. I dip into the shadows, taking cover behind a tree, praying she won't see me.

She is slouched as she kneels on the stoop, but her frame is glowing under a nearby streetlight. I focus on her familiar features, finding comfort in knowing at least one person is alive to mourn my mother.

Her striking curls are wild and frizzy, blowing softly in the night air. She looks pale and weak, exhausted from too many restless months. I imagine she hasn't slept since war broke out between the witches and vampires.

I recognize this woman as a witch from another coven, but I don't know her name. She used to visit Mamá, and together, they would talk about patrolling the town, keeping the peace. I was young, immature. I never cared to be properly introduced. I was too busy rushing off to spend time with Liv or hunt vampires.

I watch as she places a bundle of early spring flowers on the front stoop. She is crying. I can hear her sniffles from where I hide, several yards away. The wind picks up, blowing her shawl off her shoulders. She shivers and pulls the knitted garment closer, clutching it at her chest with one hand while the other traces symbols atop the front stoop. She whispers something—an apology—but I don't hear her full confession because something else distracts me. A man is approaching.

I squeeze my hands into balled fists, dangling them at my sides. I am both surprised and fearful. I want to aid the witch, rush to her side, because for all I know, this man, a stranger in town, could be the man from my dreams. After all, a new face is a rare occurrence in Darkhaven.

The woman stands, turns, and faces the intruder. "Who are you? What do you want?" she shouts. She sounds stronger than she appears.

The man flashes a badge, and I squint to see it. He moves too quickly, clasping the badge's holster shut and sliding it back into his jacket's inner pocket before I can read what it says. I groan internally.

"I'm Jackson Griggs," the man says. "I'm investigating the fire that took place at this address. Do you mind telling me what you're doing here?"

"Darkhaven is a small town, Mr. Griggs. I'm familiar with everyone, and we rarely see newcomers." The witch doesn't hide her distrust and disbelief in who he claims to be.

The man chuckles at her confession and says, "I was informed there would be quite a bit of backlash from the townspeople."

"Informed?" she asks. "By whom?"

"What are you doing here?" he asks, avoiding her question.

"Did you notice the no-trespassing signs?"

"I was leaving flowers," she says simply. She glances at the bundle sitting on the stoop.

"And you chose to ignore the no-crossing tape?" he continues. "Are you aware trespassing is against the law?"

She scoffs. "Listen here, I was good friends with the Lópezes, and I do not need permission from you—or anyone else, for that matter—to show my respect."

"You *do* need permission to visit this site, which is still under investigation," he counters.

The woman remains silent, seething as she narrows her gaze at the man. He has maneuvered himself so that only his back is to me, which is making it difficult to assess his features. From what I have seen, nothing about him appears familiar. He shares too few similarities with the man from my dream, but since I'm not one to believe in coincidences, I decide he must be tied to them. Within the span of a couple of weeks, there have been four newcomers to town: the rogue, the witch, the dreamwalker, and now the investigator. I can't ignore this, and my friends won't be able to either.

"Why are you here, Mr. Griggs?" she asks.

"Darkhaven was in need of fresh blood," he says with the hint of a smile in his voice.

The woman sucks in a breath and holds it, her gaze scanning the length of the man's tall frame. If he notices her reaction, he doesn't mention it. Still, she remains silent, waiting for the man to speak again.

"If you must know, I moved here with my younger brother. Our parents died recently, and we needed a change of scenery. It just so happens Darkhaven was hiring."

I don't like this man, and I'm fairly certain this witch

doesn't either. Something is off about him. Like Sofía, he seems to be hiding something.

"Why Darkhaven?" she asks, speaking slowly. I appreciate her interrogation, but if he really does have something to hide, he won't spill the beans tonight. I need to learn more about him, but I'm not sure how I can do that without speaking to someone in town.

"Does that matter?" he asks, crossing his arms over his chest.

The witch takes a single step backward, putting space between them. "Like I said, we aren't used to new residents. Darkhaven isn't exactly on the map."

He laughs. "I assure you, Darkhaven is on a map, and as *I* said, we were looking for a change of scenery. I was tired of city life. I wanted something . . . different. I will admit, I don't know much about small towns save for one important thing."

"And what's that?" she asks cautiously. Even from this distance, I can smell her fear.

"People tend to snoop when they should leave well enough alone," he says blatantly.

The woman's jaw clenches, brows furrowing, eyes throwing death daggers at our newest resident.

"I am *not* snooping," she says sharply. "I am showing my respect—something you need to learn more about."

The man throws up his hands in defeat. "I assure you, I have no intention of denying your right to offer condolences. I understand you were friends with the family who lived here, and I do apologize for the unfortunate incident that has brought me to Darkhaven. I wish I were here under better circumstances. But you can't disobey a clear order from the police. The tape is there for a reason. I can't properly investigate the fire if people keep breaking in."

She frowns. "What do you mean by *keep* breaking in? Someone else was here? Someone besides me?"

The man nods. "I've noticed several different individuals trespassing, which is why I thought I would stay near the property tonight."

I curse internally. He was conducting a stakeout, which can only lead to one thing: discovering I am still alive. He probably has pictures of the people who resided here, so he knows what I look like. He knows I am the daughter of the woman who died here—the very one who supposedly died with her.

I'm guessing the intruder from earlier was Jasik, when he came to gather my mother's ashes. The investigator might have even seen me here the night of the fire or when I came back the next day. I hate to admit it, but Malik was right. Returning here will only lead to disaster. If this man catches me off guard, he'll quickly discover I'm not human. In the dark, if I keep my distance, it's easy to miss my crimson eyes, my pale skin, but he's interrogating the witch up close and personal. He will definitely notice I'm inhuman.

I take several steps back, pushing away from the tree and slipping into the darkness until I'm certain they can't see me. With these two distracted by conversation, I run, abandoning the witch, dashing deeper into town and farther from the investigator.

Lunar Magic Shop is the sole occult store in Darkhaven. Surprisingly, in a town crawling with supernatural creatures, there aren't more witchy stores. Most covens harvest their own herbs, make their own candles and elixirs, and pass down their book collections, so shops like this just become a cautionary tale, another statistic to convince optimistic entrepreneurs that being your own boss isn't all it's cracked up to be.

Thankfully, the owner of this particular store brushed off the naysayers, because this is my best chance at finding out more about the amulet and the dark entity the witches created—without asking Holland.

My legs are heavy as I approach the brick building, almost like they realize how quickly this encounter can go wrong. My heart is buzzing—with excitement or fear, I'm not sure. I come to a halt, gnawing on my lower lip as I stare at the magic store.

Somewhere inside, I will find the answers I need, but I'll also find a living, breathing human being, and I don't do so well when they're nearby—you know, living, breathing, sucking up all the oxygen in the room as blood courses through their veins at unbearably high-pitched tones. It's all I can hear sometimes, and since my mug of blood is still sitting in the microwave at the manor, I should walk away. But I know I won't. I'm far too stubborn for common sense. After all, I made it this far.

Situated on a side street, the building stands two stories high, like all the downtown stores. The windows to the upstairs apartment—likely rented by yet another living, breathing person—are dark. I convince myself dark windows can mean only one of two things: the apartment is either unoccupied or currently empty. Maybe the shopkeeper lives there, and if that's the case, my total human interaction count is down to just one: whoever runs the store at night. I find comfort in this because the last thing I need is for witnesses to see me loitering in town. It would also suck if I accidentally killed said person.

The storefront is comprised of brick surrounding nearly floor-to-ceiling windows, but it is almost impossible to see inside. Words like *occult books, candles, herbs,* and *crystals* are scrawled across the glass in neat calligraphy. A hand-drawn astrology chart, with symbols to represent each sign, occupies an entire window to my left. Another pane of glass is covered in Wiccan runes, with a sign that mentions a discount if shoppers sign up for the store's email newsletter.

The door is also mostly glass, and the *Open* sign flickers brightly as I approach. I peer past the sign listing store hours, praying the time of night will ensure I am the only customer. From what I can tell, I am. It's silent, with only a single heartbeat mocking my hunger.

A dim light illuminates the checkout desk, where the clerk is reading a book, nose stuffed between the pages, completely engrossed in everything but her surroundings. She hasn't even noticed me watching her. Maybe Darkhaven wouldn't be a prime hunting spot for rogues if humans took even *basic* self-defense lessons.

Still gnawing on my lower lip, skin threatening to bleed, I try to summon the courage to enter the store. From Main Street a few yards away, I hear the echo of approaching footsteps and laughter. A couple passes by, not bothering to glance over at me. Yet another example of why rogues keep settling in this area. I shake my head as they disappear down the walkway.

When I let my mind focus on the task at hand, I enter an internal battle with Malik, an argument I will never win. I don't need the power of spirit and foresight to predict his wrath. When he finds out I came here tonight, he will be furious. But the question is, *how* furious? I've come to learn there are different levels to his anger.

At level one, Malik is still the strong, silent type. His quiet seething is somehow deafening, but he's just mad, not quite angry enough to say anything. He knows his silence speaks volumes, and that's enough.

Next, we have level two. At this point, he forgoes silence and forces me into the basement training quarters, where he proceeds to take out his frustration on me while explaining the art of war. I usually succumb to his reasoning, and I spend the rest of the night pretending the body aches are my imagination. We haven't trained in days, so I'm guessing he may skip level two and dive headfirst into what lies beyond.

Like level two, Malik's level three is verbal, but it's a different kind of loud. Instead of using metaphors and analogies on how my mistakes are comparable to failed battle plans, he expresses his disappointment in me. Honestly, this is the worst level I've experienced to date. There is nothing quite as awful as knowing you've let down someone you care about. I can handle his anger, but I can't always handle his pain.

Finally, Malik reaches level four. While I hate experiencing level three and Malik's disappointment in me, I am terrified of level four. This is the point of no return, when the mistakes are so grand, they threaten our livelihood. Malik would never physically hurt me, but while wearing his new leadership hat, I can picture him asking me to leave the manor and never return.

Somehow, deep down, I know stepping inside the magic shop, crossing that threshold, I will awaken level four in Malik. There will be no going back, and as much as that kills me, what other choice do I have? If I can't trust my friends, I have no one else to aid me but my enemies. Deciding to be impulsive, I enter the store, choosing to ignore the itchy sensation in my gut that's screaming at me to leave.

The air is coated by burning incense. I can see the smoke swirling around me, seeping into my clothes. I inhale deeply, and while the scent is a bit overwhelming, it puts me at ease. Nothing quite reminds me of home like burning sage.

The lighting overhead is a soft yellow, so dim and low I tell myself the shopkeeper may not see my crimson irises if I keep my distance. And since spring is newly emerging, I like to think everyone in Darkhaven has lost their tan.

I scan the store, which is surprisingly large for having such a small storefront. The front part of the store houses most of the items. On one side of the store, the walls are cluttered with glass jars, all labeled with names of various herbs. On the other side, I find boxes of candles in different heights and thickness, in every shade available. There are several tables scattered about, with rows of relics used for magic, from pentagrams to crystals.

The back half of the store mirrors the layout of a traditional bookstore, with several rows of shelves stacked with volumes. The smell beyond incense is that of musty old tomes, with yellowed, frayed pages. Everything about this store makes my heart happy.

A large chandelier buzzes above me, offering warm yellow lighting to guide me inside.

I make the mistake of glancing at my right, where the shopkeeper stands beside the register. A spinning carousel of Pagan-inspired jewelry is beside the front counter, and I pretend to be distracted by something to avoid looking at the girl.

"Hi there!" she calls, voice bubbly, high-pitched, and far too eager at the chance to gain a customer. Based on past experiences, I imagine her store isn't doing as well as she hoped it would.

In my effort to beeline for the books at the back of the store, I grin and nod, sidestepping a table cluttered with Lunar Magic Shop merchandise. The girl closes her book and stands straighter.

"Are you looking for anything in particular?" she asks.

I shake my head, desperate to keep as much space between us as possible. She begins to walk around the front counter, inching closer as I proceed to step backward. I bump into the wall, and glass jars of herbs clink together. I spin, probably a little too quickly, and adjust them so they don't fall. I mumble an apology.

"No worries! That is, as long as you're okay with my you-break-you-buy policy," she says, laughing. Her voice is soft and sweet, and something about the way she speaks has me turning to face her.

"Oh, I'm just kidding," she says when I don't laugh, dismissing her joke with a wave of her hand. "My name is Luna, and if you need help finding anything, just let me know."

I nod, undeniably charmed by her allure. Something about her—maybe the way she smells or the way she sounds or the way she carries herself—invites me closer. She smells like honeysuckle and dried flowers. Her hair is stick straight and jet black, with long fringe poking down behind her teal-framed glasses. Her eyes are light gray, almost silver, and even though every fiber of my body is telling me to look away, I cannot.

When she turns around, we break eye contact, and I manage to find the strength to walk away from the girl. The closer I am to the stacks, the greater the distance between us, the easier it is to ignore her. Still, as I scour book titles and author names, I find myself peering through the bookcases, trying to catch a glimpse of her.

Luna remains at the register, humming softly as she twirls a lock of hair around her index finger. She is flipping through the pages of her book, frowning as she scans the text. Something about it has disappointed her, and I want to know what that is.

I can hear her heartbeat, strong and steady, and it makes my stomach churn. Her skin, smooth and milky, is radiant in the low lighting. Something sparkles at her clavicle, and I focus on it. The glint of a crescent moon, bright silver, glows back at me.

Behind the front desk, there is a large clock adorned with astrology symbols instead of numbers. It is nearly nine at night. It's late for the store to be open, so I assume it will soon close. There are no customers, and the lighting seems dark and moody, even for a metaphysical shop, like maybe Luna was in the process of closing before I showed up. Regardless, I probably don't have much time. I need to find what I came for.

Luna looks up, catching my eyes, and I look away quickly. I turn, scanning the shelf behind me. I hear her approach. Internally, I try to calm myself. The only thing worse than admitting to Malik that I came here is also mentioning the untimely death of the shopkeeper. He will be none too pleased with me. And even though I remind myself of this, even though I tell myself she will notice my crimson irises if I face her, I want to turn around, to greet her fully, to relish in her scent and understand just what I find so familiar about her.

Thankfully, I don't do this. At least there is a part of me, however small, that has kept my wits about me.

"Are you looking for a particular text?" she asks.

She is standing so close, *too close*. Her scent washes over me, filling my lungs with honey and lavender. I hold my breath, shake my head again, and squeeze my eyes shut, silently willing her away. If she notices my distress, she doesn't mention it.

Please go away. Please. Please. Please!

"If you have an idea of what you're looking for, maybe I can lead you in the right direction," she offers.

Realizing she won't allow me to simply browse on my own—I suppose it is too late for that—I open my eyes and steady my breath with slow, calm exhalations. I keep my gaze on the stacks before me. I am diligent as I scan the spines, noting every single title, every single author name.

"I—uh—I'm looking for something about crystals," I say, never glancing over.

"Oh! I have some wonderful texts on crystals. Are you a beginner?" she asks.

"The history of crystals. Maybe magical uses," I say, ignoring her query. I try to remain as vague as possible because asking for books on the dark arts must raise red flags.

"You know, I just got a really interesting book in stock. It's an older text. It has some modern-day uses for crystals, but it focuses mainly on historical uses from cultures all over the world. Perhaps that will interest you?"

I nod, relieved. An old text about the use of crystals in ancient cultures must have the answer to my predicament. Perhaps if I find out more about the amulet and the dark entity, Malik will forgive me this one discretion.

"Yes, that sounds like exactly what I'm looking for," I say.

"Great! Let me just grab it from the back room. I haven't

completely unpacked my latest shipment."

Again, I nod, pretending to be distracted by the other books in front of me. I finger the spines, attempting to look deep in thought. I'm certain I am failing miserably, but the shopkeeper disappears into the back room and returns a few minutes later with a beefy, leather-bound book in her arms. She cradles it to her chest as she approaches me.

I keep my eyes lidded, gaze pointed downward, hoping it's enough to hide my irises. It must be, because she never mentions them.

"I'll take it," I say quickly.

"Don't you want to take a look at it first?" she asks. "I don't mind if you peruse the pages before purchasing. It might not be what you're looking for, and I do have other texts on crystals."

I peer up, glancing at the tome. As much as I am itching to leave, she's right. I have to be sure the book indeed has the information I need, so I nod, taking the book from her hands and scanning the cover.

"I'll be at the register," Luna says before walking away.

When she's behind the counter, fully engrossed in her book, I can finally breathe. Being around humans is *exhausting*. I have no intention of doing this again, so I need to be sure I find everything I'm looking for.

I sit, legs crossed, as I search the book's table of contents page. Not finding anything of real value, I flip to the back and check the index. When I find a section labeling different types of crystals, I search for black onyx, holding my breath the whole time. When I find it, I flip to the correct section.

Scanning each page printed in neat, tiny letters, I find not just what I'm looking for but also so much more.

*Black onyx is a powerful protection stone used to absorb
and transform negative energy. It also helps to prevent the
drain of personal energy.*

This makes sense. Mamá said she wore that particular
crystal for protection. Being a powerful spirit user, she would
only need protection from negative energy—something we
can't always see. She could protect herself from physical
threats but not invisible threats.

*Black onyx is also used for meditation and dreaming.
When using black onyx for either of these purposes, it
is recommended to use a secondary grounding stone in
combination with black onyx. When used properly, black
onyx can help the user become master of their own future.*

I reread that passage again while thinking about my own
dreams. Ever since I took control of the amulet, my nightmares
have been more vivid, more raw and real, and I am dreaming
about the past more often than I used to. It's getting harder to
decipher what is a dream or nightmare and what is a vision.

I grab on to the crystal, feeling it warm against my hand.
I wear the amulet to bed every night, too afraid to remove it
when I'm at my most vulnerable, and if this passage is correct,
it *is* influencing me, just like Malik fears.

*Additionally, black onyx aids the development of emotional
and physical strength and stamina, especially when
support is needed during times of stress, confusion, grief,
or transformation.*

I frown. *Transformation?* What does it mean by

transformation? Still holding the amulet, I bring the crystal to my lips. My skin tingles at the contact, but I am too engrossed to pull away.

Every ancient culture believed in the power of black onyx. Ancient Egyptians believed black onyx caused detachment between the body and the soul. It also aided transformation by treating the blood disorder. It is said to strengthen life, from the heart to the nerves to the blood, expelling evil.

Similarly, black onyx was popular among the ancient Greeks. Black onyx was such a prominent crystal in Ancient Greece, a fable was passed down through the generations. Onyx is the Greek word for nail or claw. Ancient Greeks believed darkness used its claws to cut the divine flesh of Venus while she was sleeping. Her blood scattered across the sand, so the fates turned the mixture into stone so that no part of the heavenly body would ever perish. This is what formed the black onyx crystal, and it is believed to be the only stone capable of returning ash to earth and restore the spirit, eliminating darkness and restoring light.

I suck in a sharp breath, rereading the fable over and over again, unbelieving of what it says. I continue on with bated breath.

Because of the black onyx's power, it has been used in the black arts to summon evil spirits and dark entities capable of possession. But if used properly, only the black onyx crystal has the power to vanquish this evil and restore the soul.

A knot has formed in my throat, threatening to steal my very breath. As terrified as I am, I cannot avert my gaze. It is glued to the words, soaking in the information shared on these aged, yellowing pages.

The use of black onyx is painfully clear. While the stone's power is abused by those who dabble in the dark arts, it was meant for greater things. I was born into magic and have used it all my life, but it still has the ability to leave me awestruck at its capabilities.

It is believed to be the only stone capable of returning ash to earth and restore the spirit, eliminating darkness and restoring light.

Perhaps my coven was onto something when they completed that dark spell to sever my vampire half. But in focusing too much on their own incantation, they failed. If only they'd properly harnessed the power of black onyx, there just might have been a way to restore my humanity after all.

I close the book and run my palm over the stiff, aged cover. Without title or author name, this tome looks more like an old grimoire passed down through the family than published nonfiction. Solidifying my assumption, the only thing adorning the front cover is a symbol. Burned into the leather, leaving a dark crease in its wake, there is a cross, but instead of the top arm, there is a loop. I trace the circle with my fingertips, a rush of energy surging through me.

. . . returning ash to earth and restore the spirit . . .

I swallow hard, forcing the knot into my esophagus. It sits against my chest, carving a hole where my heart once was. I replay the words over and over again, rewinding the reel even when I feel I cannot continue.

. . . eliminating darkness and restoring light.

"You were right, Mamá," I whisper, speaking so softly I'm not sure I even spoke at all.

Black onyx is capable of more than simply containing an evil entity summoned by misguided witches. This crystal has the power to cure vampirism.

THREE

The moon above is full and bright, cascading streams of light to illuminate my way. I stare at her, engrossed in her beauty, in her power. So often, witches use the moon's strength to fuel their spells, to force a change summoned by their will alone. If she could speak, would she tell them she is ashamed by their use of her magic? Would she be disappointed in me, in my past reckless behavior?

I sigh, glancing away, no longer able to face her. I kick at the ground, frustrated by all that I have learned. The book, thick and long, is weighty in my arms. I hold on to it tightly, thinking about the power of knowledge passed down through generations of families. I wonder who wrote this book and how long ago that was. More importantly, how did it end up at an occult shop in Darkhaven? It arrived the same day I needed it, and that alone is alarming.

Even though I reread the passages about black onyx until it was clear Luna wanted to close the store, I still can't believe the witches were right about vampirism being treatable. Clearly, this book was the final puzzle piece they needed— the very one they didn't consult when they completed their spell. If they had read this book and used its knowledge while performing the dark spell, they would have cured us.

But what does that mean? That means they wouldn't have

shown up at dawn. There wouldn't have been that final battle. Will would be alive. Amicia would be alive. My mother would be alive. Instead, we *all* fell at the hands of the ill-informed. Rash in their decisions, the witches rushed to harness magic they knew nothing about. And it cost them their lives.

Part of me wants to hold on to my anger, to hold a grudge against the people who wronged me, even if they did pay the ultimate price. I am ashamed of this desire, but simply being aware of shameful behavior isn't enough to extinguish the spark fueling that fire. I need to find a way to forgive them—to *really, truly* forgive them for what they did.

The subtle snap of twigs breaking under weight catches my attention. I peer into the distance. The forest seems to go on for miles and miles. It ends in darkness, blurring together, too murky for even my heightened senses to see what lies beyond.

I hold the book tighter, knowing I must keep it safe. I was supposed to be patrolling these woods tonight. Earlier, I was eager for a fight, but now, the thought of endangering what may be our sole chance at finding a cure leaves me on edge. I can't risk damaging the contents inside. Already ripe with age, the book is on the brink of decay, pages yellowed and crisp like autumn leaves. It would never survive being tossed around by a careless rogue vampire.

Just as I am about to make a run for the manor, Jasik steps out from the shadows, eyeing me curiously. I imagine myself from his point of view: clinging hopelessly to a book, gaze darting around in sheer panic, foot burrowing into the soil as I intend to push off and run away. I feel sweat beading at my forehead, hear my heartbeat thumping within my mind. I definitely don't look like a hunter patrolling the forest for rogue vampires. I look more like prey than predator.

"Ava," Jasik says cautiously. He glances around, assessing the situation like a true hunter. "What's wrong?"

He is looking for a would-be attacker. Everything about my demeanor worries him. If the situation were reversed, he would be worrying me too. I consider being clever, trying to wit my way out of this, but I resort to honesty.

"Nothing," I say. I offer a weak chuckle, hoping to ease his tension. I doubt it works. "I wasn't expecting you. You startled me." I shrug nonchalantly.

"You left so quickly," he says. "I wanted to make sure you were okay."

"I'm sorry about that. I just . . . " I swallow hard. "I needed space."

Jasik nods, breaking eye contact. "Because of the memorial. I'm sorry if I overstepped. I thought—"

"No," I say. My voice is squeaky as I speak too loudly, too quickly. "That meant so much to me."

He smiles softly, his crimson irises sparkling in the moonlight. I know he believes me from the glint of happiness in his eyes.

"You have to have an outlet, a way to speak to her, to mourn her," he says. "And it's important that you know it's okay to miss them, even after everything they did."

I nod and stare at the ground. I focus on the dirt, on the dry granules that have softened with the emergence of a warmer season. Early spring flowers are beginning to bloom, and with their growth, the scent of the dead will dissipate. I will finally be able to take a full, deep breath without being reminded of all I lost. Even now, the lingering stench of death is all around me. It fills my chest, making it almost too heavy to breathe.

"I feel alone," I confess, voice soft.

Tears are only a blink away, but I force down that emptiness, choking on my words as my heart nearly implodes in my chest. As a vampire, I am gifted with enhancement in every way, including emotional duress.

Jasik closes the space between us. I lean against him, still clutching the book to my chest, as he wraps his arms around me. I bury my face in his shirt, nuzzling between the zipper of his jacket. I inhale his familiar scent—blood and mint. The steady beat of his heart comforts my own, even as it breaks.

We stand like this for a long time, both unwilling to speak, both unsure of what to say even if we wanted to crack the silence. There is nothing quite like facing an eternity all alone. Jasik has Malik, his biological brother, but I have no one. Nothing but friends who constantly threaten to oust me. Nothing but nestmates who believe a suspicious newcomer over me.

"I promise you will never be alone," Jasik whispers, breath fluttering the hair atop my head. "I will be here, Ava. Always."

I shake my head, pushing myself even harder against his muscular frame. He holds me firmly, a solid slab of impenetrable steel. I feel safe in his arms, like he alone could keep me from the world and all its problems.

"You can't promise that," I mumble against his chest.

"I have been alive a long time," he says. "I am pretty good at surviving."

I want to believe him, but the world is cruel. There will come a time when Jasik will be forced to choose: his brother or me. The only happiness I find in that is knowing I won't be the one making him choose. Malik will. I make a lot of mistakes, and even though I always have the best intentions, Malik will believe he has no other choice but to cast me away. Maybe leaving is best. Maybe I am better off on my own, risking no other neck but my own.

I push away from Jasik, letting the space between us strengthen my wobbly legs, my jelly spine, my weakening desire to return to the manor. I risk a glance at my sire, but he isn't looking at me. He is staring at the book in my arms. When he catches me looking at him, he finally speaks.

"What do you have?" he asks.

"A book," I say carefully. I hold on to it so tightly I think I may imprint the shape of my arms into the leather cover.

"Where did you get it from?" he asks, frowning.

"I, uh, I went back," I say.

"To your old house?" he asks, shocked.

I nod.

"But why?" he asks. "I brought her ashes to you so you wouldn't have to go back."

"I know, but I . . . I had to get this. It's a family heirloom."

"I'm surprised it survived the fire," he says. His gaze flickers between the book and my eyes.

"We got lucky," I say.

My voice is whisper-soft, and even I don't believe the lie I have just told. But something about my resolve must have silenced Jasik, because he doesn't question my story. Or perhaps he is going to let the others complete his dirty work. They too will notice the book, and when Malik finds out, I will be forced to confess.

"Next time, let me go with you," he says. "It's safer that way."

"I won't be going back," I say firmly.

I think about the investigator and the visiting witch, but I don't mention them. Eventually, I will come clean, but I'd like another night of peace.

"I know it's not fair, but never returning is for the best," he says.

"I know," I say.

He glances at the sky. "We should get back to the manor. Only a few hours until sunrise."

Jasik and I stand at the edge of our property. The cemetery is several yards away, and I stare at the rows of headstones marking lost souls. I see them every day, and it's no easier. It doesn't even make it feel more real. There are times I wake and I forget. Will is alive. Amicia is here. My mother is at home, learning to build a life without a husband and child. But then I remember.

"It still hurts," I admit.

Jasik is beside me. We didn't speak the rest of the walk home, and with the book in my arms, it took twice as long to navigate the unkempt trails. Jasik suggested he carry the book, but I made excuses every time he offered. Now, he seems on edge, clearly confused by my reluctance, but instead of being direct, he bottled up his concern—like we all do.

"I know," he says. "Time will ease the pain."

"Good thing we're immortal. We're just *oozing* with time," I say, voice laced with my annoyance.

I am tired of being told that time heals all. That if I just wait long enough, I will forget how much I cared. Am I the only one who doesn't want to forget them?

"Are you sure you're okay?" Jasik asks.

I can feel his gaze on me, but I don't look at him. I keep my vision focused on the tombstones ahead. I glance at my mother's. A mound of fresh dirt catches my eye. Jasik must have buried her ashes after I left. I'm both grateful and bothered by this.

"Jasik, can I ask you something?"

"Of course," he says. "You can ask me anything."

"Would you want to be human again?"

He exhales sharply, likely surprised by my question. He is quiet for a long time. I don't rush him. I need his honest answer.

The silence stretches on, and when I finally glance up at him, I see the anger and confusion in his eyes even as he tries to hide it.

"Would you take the cure?" I ask.

He shakes his head, averting his gaze. His eyes are hard now, and he won't look at me.

"What is it?" I ask. "What's wrong?"

"I . . ." He sighs heavily, running a hand through his already tousled hair. "I'm surprised. Where is this coming from? You fought so hard to become a vampire, to reverse the curse the witches cast on you. And now you're treating vampirism like it's a virus that can be cured."

"No, this isn't about that. I just . . . I need to know. If you could, would you give up immortality? Would you take a cure and be human again?"

"Don't you think it's finally time that you accept what you are?" Jasik asks.

Pain flashes in his eyes, and I realize my question has hurt him. I never meant to seem ungrateful for the life he offered me, even though I always manage to appear that way.

Not waiting for my response, Jasik walks away,

disappearing into the manor and leaving me outside. Alone.

"You never answered my question," I whisper. I know he doesn't hear me because he's already gone.

I kneel before her, sinking into the soft earth. My legs burrow deeply as I sit on my heels. I wipe away debris that has landed atop her stone, and I stare at the name etched in granite.

Tatiana López

My mother.

The box that carried her ashes from her house to this resting place is gone. Jasik likely brought it inside, leaving it for me in my bedroom. He knows how important it is to me, and he wouldn't want it to remain buried, decomposing with everything else beneath this lawn.

"I do forgive you, Mamá," I say. "I just wish you would have . . ."

I sigh heavily, expelling every wisp of breath until my lungs spasm in protest. My chest aches, heaving as I suck in oxygen too quickly. I desire the pain because it reminds me I'm alive. I made it this far. Regardless of everything the world has thrown at me since I became a vampire, I am still here.

"I don't know what to say," I confess. "That's what makes this so hard."

I set down the book, tracing the ankh cross with my fingertips. The edges are rough, the leather tight and wrinkled. I bet it was once smooth, but that was a long time ago.

The worst part of losing someone is being forced to move

on without them. There is a massive, gaping hole in my life, and I am supposed to fill it with other things—as if a new hobby or friend can replace what used to reside there.

I can't escape it either. Everywhere I go, I see the hole. I see it at night in my bedroom, when my mom used to wish me sweet dreams. I see it in the kitchen at breakfast, when my mom used to cook for me. I see it at dinnertime, when my mom used to ask me about my day. I see it in my dreams, my nightmares, when I'm awake or asleep. That silent, dark abyss is everywhere I go.

It takes a form, morphing into the short, slender silhouette of my mother, and it follows me around, stealing the tiny bit of sanity I have left and replacing it with anguish.

"I might have read the words myself, with my own two eyes, but somehow, that doesn't make them more believable." I sigh sharply, loudly. "I still can't believe you were right."

My gaze is focused on the book. The cover is dark, bumpy, and when I open it, the spine protests, cracking. I cringe internally at the sound it makes.

Marked by the years, the pages are crisp and tea-stained. I flip through, careful not to damage the pages I have yet to read. I stop when I reach the chapter about black onyx crystals.

I flatten my palm against the pages, feeling them give way at the spine. A crease forms, keeping the book open as I focus on the words written. I reread what I learned earlier today, still silenced by their truth.

A long moment passes as I let what I have learned sink in. It seems impossible, to have a cure, a way back to the light. Jasik doesn't want to look at vampirism as a virus, a plague against humanity, but it seems that's exactly what it is. One bite and infection spreads.

Contrary to what my sire believes, I have accepted my fate, and I hate that it has come to this. Ignoring what I have learned would be a disservice to every vampire turned against his or her will. If there is a cure, I must find it—if not for myself, then for them, for anyone who needs it.

The longer I sit outside, poring over every page contained within the covers of this book, the worse I feel. I noticed it earlier today when I left the manor. The farther away I walked, the better I felt, like this place is cloaked in darkness and the weight of it hangs tightly to my chest. When I'm here, I feel crazy and paranoid, and even though I tell myself this all must be a figment of my imagination, I find my gaze darting around the property, stealing glances at the shadows, certain that something lurks within them. I no longer feel in control of my eyes. Like my heart, which beats rapidly on its own, my eyes scan my surroundings and my mind tells them to be wary.

The amulet hanging from my neck is weighty against my skin. The tiny hairs there prickle each time it sways when I move, alerting me to its presence. I don't need the reminder that this crystal is dangerous or that it is my responsibility to keep it safe until I can find a way to properly exorcise the evil within.

I grasp it. For something that holds the power of an entire coven and the essence of a dark entity, it feels entirely too small. The scratchy edges are crude against my palm. Clasping my hand closed, I use my fingertips to turn it over in my hand. Each time it moves, something jolts through my arm and down my spine. It stings, vibrating outward into my flesh.

I *hate* this amulet. I hate that I am the one burdened by its power, but most of all, I hate that I can't just get rid of it. I would love nothing more than to walk to the edge of the sea and toss it over the ledge, watching as it sinks into the murky, watery depths.

Even if I were certain no one would find it, I still wouldn't toss it over. I need this crystal. Without it, there is no cure. Somehow, I think the darkness inside is aware of that. It laughs at my pain, self-assured that I will do everything in my power to keep it close to me even as it drains me of my sanity and strength.

I drop it, lowering my arm until I touch the ground. I reposition and cross my legs. I close my eyes, grounding myself by drawing energy and strength from the earth. I loosen the tightness in my muscles and breathe slowly, inhaling through my nose and exhaling through my mouth. I let the air linger a bit, feeling it swirl round and round in my lungs.

The elements are all around me, and I take refuge in their presence. From the warm, salty air to the softening, cool ground, I summon them, but the moment they enter my body, threading through the weakest parts of me, the amulet at my chest begins to burn.

When it gets too hot, I take in a breath of air, hissing at the fiery contact. I release the elements and brush the amulet off my skin, rubbing the damage done. My flesh is raw but heals quickly.

Still dangling from a chain, the black onyx crystal simply sways from side to side, never relinquishing its hold.

"I'll find a way to destroy you once and for all," I say, an edge of deadly threat in my tone.

I stand, wiping dirt from my jeans, and I grab the book, holding it close to my chest. I glance over my shoulder at the woods in the distance. The sky is growing light, a promise of the upcoming sunrise, yet even as the earth begins to warm and the sky brightens, something dark is at play. I feel it in the air, and it makes my skin prickle with worry.

I face the house, and as I walk closer to the manor, something catches my eye. Curtains in Jasik's bedroom flutter, and the shadow of an eavesdropper falls out of sight. I narrow my gaze, assuming the culprit is none other than our newest houseguest.

"*Sofía*," I whisper, voice laced with my hatred of the girl.

And at the mention of her name, the crystal buzzes with excitement.

In the kitchen, I open the microwave, finding it empty. I expected this, but I am surprisingly disappointed. If it were still there, I couldn't drink it. After sitting out for hours, the blood would be too spoiled to consume. I may not die from tainted blood, but I can certainly get an upset stomach ... I think.

I sigh, shuffling over to the refrigerator and grabbing a fresh blood bag. I tear it open with my teeth, relishing in the savagery of my hunger, as I search the cabinets for a mug. Some blood drips down my chin, and I swipe it clean with my tongue. Cup in hand, I spill the liquid contents inside and place it in the microwave.

"Nothing quite like a bedtime snack with a side of radiation poisoning," Sofía says.

I hear her enter the kitchen, the door leading to the butler's pantry swooshing closed behind her. Trapped in this small space, my senses home in on her, even if I am desperate to ignore her intrusion.

I remain facing the cabinets, gaze glued to the time on the microwave, watching as it slowly ticks downward. Is it just me, or are the seconds passing by slower than usual?

"Everyone is asleep," Sofía says. Her voice is soft, playful almost. From her reflection in the microwave, I can see she is grinning.

My hands are balled into fists, arms dangling at my sides, and I squeeze them tighter. I dig my nails into my skin, focusing on the biting pain as I nearly bleed. This is a trick I have used many times now. It helps me concentrate, giving my senses something else to worry about. I am a hunter, so the threat of being harmed should take full priority over anything else. But this time, it doesn't work.

Sofía is quiet for a brief, peaceful moment. I close my eyes, steadying my breathing, but with each inhalation, I smell her. And she smells like magic, like what my mother used to smell like. Witches have a particular scent. They smell like sage and mugwort and just about any magical herb available to them. They smell like the elements, like water and fire and earth. The scent is ingrained so deeply, they can never wash it away. It is one with them, much like their elemental control.

I swallow hard, desperate to remain silent, because the moment I turn, the moment I speak up, I will lose what little control I have managed to hold on to. I know facing her will be the death of the trust the other hunters have bestowed upon me. They are starting to see Sofía as an ally, so I can't make any rash, permanent decisions until they see the truth.

The microwave is almost done nuking my supper. Only ten seconds remain.

The witch is still eerily silent behind me, and as unsettling as that is, I am grateful for the peace. Every time she speaks, her voice lashes out at me. My skin is raw from her beatings.

I am beginning to shake, so I hold my breath. Every fiber of my body is shouting for me to turn around. My skin prickles and my hair stands on end. I release the breath I was holding, and it comes out shaky and loud. I think I hear her snicker, but I don't respond. I don't even look her way.

I open the microwave three seconds too soon and grab the mug. It is hot in my palm, and I wince at the stabbing pain. I gulp down the scalding liquid, throat burning at the abrupt, harsh contact. When I'm finished, I set down the mug on the counter so quick, so hard, it almost shatters. A deep line worms its way up the side, cracking the ceramic. I turn and toss it into the nearby trash can, not bothering to check if it's fixable.

I wait before turning around, but even with blood in my system, I feel no better. My hunger is squashed, that empty pit sated, but I don't feel revitalized. I know I feel this way because of Sofía. For some reason, it is easier being around witches than humans, but it isn't at all easy being around *her*. I would rather be back at that shop, peering at Luna through the stacks like a sociopath, than . . .

I suddenly realize why the witch has been silent for so long. I was naïve enough to believe she offered me mercy.

I spin on my heels, finding Sofía engrossed in the book I left on the table across the room. She is smiling coyly, fingers grazing the cover. She traces the ankh symbol, hands mirroring what my own did not even an hour ago.

She blinks, and I am at her side. I grab on to her hand, tightening my grasp. Her bones are fragile beneath my own, and I find myself squeezing harder rather than releasing her. It is a risk. I have little self-control as it is, and the hunter within me is itching to lunge outward. Something deep down snaps, and I am eager to harm the girl.

She sucks in a loud breath and holds it, no doubt overwhelmed by the budding pain I am causing. She keeps her gaze focused on mine, but where hers betrays her fear, I am certain mine does not. Because Sofía doesn't scare me. In fact, I am rather quite intrigued by her now. I like to play games, and I like to win.

"You are on dangerous ground, Sofía," I say.

I glance at the book. Her gaze follows my own, and I know she understands my warning.

"I don't like to share," I remind her.

"Let me go," she hisses, emphasizing each word.

"Don't. Test. Me," I warn, mimicking her troubled pauses.

I know she is scared. I can smell it. It overpowers her natural musk and permeates all around us. She is smart to be scared. Something inside her is telling her that something inside me is stronger. She may think me a monster, but she forgets that monsters are far more wicked than witches.

"You would never win this fight," I say, and I smile.

For the first time in a long time, I *feel* my smile. From my lips to my soul, I grin at her, blissfully sure and undeniably pleased with how this has progressed in my favor. The witch is no match for this hybrid, for I have the devil at my fingertips. As I think this, the amulet warms, soothing the parts of me that once worried I am too reckless.

All at once, the air in the room intensifies. It is stagnant, a stark contrast to the coolness that just surrounded us. Sweat dribbles down my forehead, and it becomes hard to breathe. The air thickens, and the mist coats my lungs. I hold my breath, fearful that breathing will only cause me to hack. And hacking shows weakness. Hacking lets her know I am affected by her fire magic. I refuse to grant her power over me. I refuse to let her think, even if just for a second, that she could win this battle.

"The only reason you are still alive is because I allow it," I say, never blinking.

Sofía gasps at my honesty, gaze dropping to the amulet at my chest. It is so warm it sizzles and crackles against my skin. The buzzing from within the crystal echoes around us, growing louder and louder with each exasperated breath. Sofía winces as it intensifies, and she squeezes her eyes shut at the ruckus my little demon is creating.

I lean into her, inhaling deeply as she squirms beneath my grasp. Moaning, I ruffle her hair with my nose, taking deeper breaths, enjoying as I make her more and more uncomfortable. I exhale sharply, and she shivers. My breath, coming from the dead, is likely cool against her skin, which is burning hot. I imagine that sensation is all she can think about right now.

"I want to watch as the others kill you," I whisper against her ear.

"They wouldn't," she says. Even though her voice cracks, her certainty is overly confident. It annoys me.

"They will," I say adamantly. "When they realize you are not a friend, they will have no choice but to consider you a threat."

Sofía yelps as I dig my fingers into her flesh. There is no space between us. With our noses nearly touching, we stare into each other's eyes. The position is intimate in all the best ways—predator lurking over prey, certain of ambush.

"What makes you think you can take me?" she says.

I smile even wider, discovering I have a new emotion for the girl: admiration. I respect her confidence, and if things were different, we may have been friends. But that will never happen now.

I laugh, heavy and loud, a deep bellow that resonates from my gut. It sounds nothing like me, but I give it no thought. It startles Sofía, but with my hand still keeping her in place, she cannot run.

"I could use my fire magic right now," she says, voice shaky. "You would burn."

"And like the phoenix, I will rise from the ashes," I say. "But will you? Because if I'm on fire, you'll burn too."

I don't wait for a response. I simply release her, grabbing my book and exiting the kitchen, all the while humming the melody to a song resounding from the black onyx crystal.

FOUR

I am standing in the middle of a street. When I first got here, the sight was unfamiliar to me, but the longer I linger, the more I see. The haze clears, the mist settles, and I realize I am in Darkhaven.

The pavement is black and cool against my feet. I am without shoes, wearing only a nightgown—one I am certain I do not own. It is sheer and white, and I feel every breeze.

I shiver, even when the wind calms and the world is still. I shiver because I am not alone.

I see something in the distance. The silhouette of a man. He is tall and slender. His arms dangle at his sides, and his fingers seem to stretch on endlessly. They blur into the darkness at his feet.

I think he is floating. I angle my head, trying to get a better look. But when I blink, he is closer. No longer hovering above the pavement, he approaches me confidently. I fear him, but he does not fear me.

He speaks to me, I think. Does he say my name? The sound is soft and raspy, like he is intentionally manipulating his voice. Maybe he is. Maybe I know his true identity, so I stare longer.

I want to call to him, to ask for his name or order him to stop, but I have fallen mute. I try again and fail.

I clutch my throat, desperate to make a sound, *any* sound at all. But I choke on the ragged huff that escapes my lips. When I cough, it is silent, yet I still feel the convulsions in my chest, the rapid squeeze of my lungs. They too search for the breath that will set me free.

I take a step backward, just a single, small step, but it feels like I have walked a mile. The soles of my feet burn. The pavement, no longer cool, no longer new, begins to crack from wear. Before my eyes, it is as though years pass, not seconds. What was once black and smooth is now gray and chipped.

I shield my eyes as I glance at the sky. My skin is hot, sweat glistening under rays, hair clinging to my forehead. I feel weighty and full and sticky.

The sun is overhead, yet the world is dark. Shadows sway as if they are alive. They stretch outward, consuming the street. They morph into shapes, curving around lampposts, sliding over the roadway. Like the man who stares from the distance, the night gloom watches me. I never knew it was possible for shadows to have eyes.

Unsure of what to do to stop their ascent, I lift my arms before me as if I can cast these intruders away with the flick of my wrist, but my limbs are heavy. It feels like bags of stones have been tied to my fingers and I am sinking deep into the sea, surrounded by nothing but the obsidian-colored depths. I used to like the water, but now it silences my cries.

I am still standing in the road, so I know I am not drowning. I glance down, hoping my vision will ground me in this place. I stare at my hands. They are coated in blood. I gasp. The blood intensifies, running wild down my body, soaking my nightgown.

I look at the man, believing he is to blame, and I know

he is smiling at me. I cannot see his face, yet I recognize his pleasure. It radiates from him, surging forward, a steady tide threatening to overpower my weakening legs. He is happy for me, but why?

The man points at me, his arms long and squirming like jelly. A single finger slithers forward, extending far beyond his natural reach. He points from me to the ground and back again. He repeats this until my gaze follows the motion.

The street is overrun with bodies. All faces blurred and unrecognizable. A torrent of blood gushes down the road, spewing toward me. The crimson river splashes against my feet, and I am ankle deep.

"*Taste it,*" the man says, voice whisper-soft and infernal.

I suck in a sharp breath, but I only succeed in alerting my senses to the feast at my toes.

"*Taste it,*" he says again, this time speaking slower, emphasizing each word.

He pleads with me, desperate for my obedience, but I also understand this to be an order. He won't leave unless I taste it, and the worst part is, I *want* to obey him. I want to drink so badly.

My mouth is dry, but the longer I think about the blood at my heels, the more my mouth begins to water, rejuvenating my tongue, which is so dry it is nearly a useless husk.

"*Drink,*" he beckons.

My eyes are wide, vision glued to the sight around me.

The town is on fire. Crumbled buildings lie in heaps along the edge of the street. Mounds of brick and shattered glass and scorched wood cage me in place.

The smoke is strong and thick and heavy in my lungs. I am desperate for fresh air, but each seething lungful promises sudden death, not life.

The burning scent of Darkhaven collapsing irritates my vision, which has become cloudy from the haze. The world is bright orange, and the heat is like a blanket against my skin. It is so strong, so lifelike, as it clings to my body.

The man points at the river of blood, and I understand that life only comes from death. To survive the fire, I must feed. I must do as he asks.

I kneel, sinking into it, and I scoop a mouthful into my palms. It streams through my fingers, my hands weak and shaky. I pool more, and this time, I successfully bring it to my lips. I drink long and deep until my stomach is so full I can't possibly drink any more.

"*How does it taste?*" he whispers, breath hot against my neck.

I feel him right behind me, long, tentacle fingers lingering on my shoulders, but when I look up, he is still in front of me, waiting in the distance.

"You shouldn't drink that," someone says, distracting me. I see the anger flash across the man's face as I turn away from him and look at the speaker.

As I spin, the world changes. No longer set ablaze, Darkhaven is renewed, buildings erect and fire smothered. The extinguished heat no longer licks my raw flesh, and I am grateful for even a moment of reprieve.

The girl beside me is young. Maybe nine. Maybe ten. Maybe even younger than that. Her hair is long and dark, and it hangs messily at her shoulders. Her eyes are bright—the color of dark honey—and full of promise. Her skin is scraped and bruised from play, but she smiles at me, the pain gone. And when she plops down beside me, toys in hand, the river of blood evaporates.

"Do you remember what you told me?" she asks.

I don't respond because I don't believe she is speaking to me. I just watch her, fascinated by such a brave child. She thinks she knows me, recognizes my face, but she doesn't. She has no idea that I am the monster she always feared.

She has a doll in her arm, and she holds it in front of her. She stares at the doll, adjusting her dress, which has become crooked from being carried under the girl's arm.

The doll has bright-red hair braided in pigtails. A light-blue bow rests to one side, and the color of the bow matches the doll's skirt. Its shirt was once white, but now it's almost gray, like it has been dropped too many times in the dirt.

The girl holds the doll with both hands, her fingers wrapping around each of the doll's arms. She places the doll's feet on the ground and pretends to walk it around us. All the while, the girl is humming loudly. The tune is lighthearted and fast, a pretty melody for such a pretty girl.

"Do you remember what you told me?" she repeats, but this time her lips don't move. She is still humming to herself, gaze focused on her toy.

I decide to answer her by shaking my head. She isn't looking at me, but I think she understands my response.

I want to reach for her, to touch her smooth, milky-soft skin, but I do not. I fear she will leave if I do. And I am desperate not to lose her.

"You promised we would be safe," she says. She plops onto her bottom and clutches her doll to her chest. "You said we would always be okay."

I swallow hard, a knot forming in my throat. My tongue is once again dry, and my innards crave the blood flowing in her veins. But I just drank. I fed only moments ago. Why do I crave her blood, her innocence?

I can't feed from this girl because I know her all too well.

"Ava," I whisper to the girl, talking to the sweet, young, pure soul I used to be.

I was virtuous then. Moral and honest. A young mortal witch who knew nothing of the dangers lurking in this world. I always feared monsters were under my bed, and in my worst nightmares, I imagined I would become one. I was right.

"Will you keep your promise this time?" she asks, no longer looking at her doll.

She stares at me, eyes wide and dripping with tears. Her cheeks are flushed, and the steady beats of her heart tease my control.

I cannot respond. I try to speak, to convince her that we will make it through this, just as I have always told myself when things get hard, but once again, I am mute. I am silenced by the monster.

The man is behind her now, and I scream. I shriek for her to run, but young and feeble, she doesn't move in time. She simply stares at me, and I watch the exact moment she dies.

The man slices through her small, frail body, cutting through flesh. The snap of skin ripping, the squish of muscle tearing, and the crack of bones breaking resonates in my mind, penetrating my heart. I am sprayed, soaked in her blood.

The man laughs as I lunge forward, grabbing on to the child. I rock back and forth, breathing rapidly. The loud bursts calm my mind as I am overrun with one simple emotion: agony. I mourn the death of this child, the elimination of her innocence.

I cradle her in my arms, holding the torn pieces of her body together, but she is a puzzle I can't finish. She is gone now, and I can't put her back together.

The harder I hold on to her, the faster she disappears. Even though I am aware of this, I can't relinquish my grasp. I want to keep her safe, to protect her from the monster, but she leaves me. The child is gone, but I am not alone.

"You're never alone," he says softly.

I lean back, sitting on my heels. The tears flow freely, sliding down my face and splashing against my thighs.

I stare at the ground, believing I can will her back to me if I try hard enough, but all I succeed in doing is summoning the sea of blood. It returns to me, and my own tears wash away in its waves.

"You did this," I say, voice hard and angry. "You will pay for this."

The man laughs, a loud, barking bellow that surrounds me. The noise is deafening, so I clutch my head between my hands, covering my ears. I scratch my fingernails against my scalp and begin to rock. I hum the girl's tune, but I sit here for a long time before the melody finally overpowers the man's menacing chuckle.

"Ava?" someone says.

I open my eyes. The blood is gone. I lower my hands and gently touch the ground. It feels real and strong, no longer caving under the weight of the monster's nightmare.

I glance up, and I see her. The girl I have seen before in another dream. She was unrecognizable then, but this time her face is fully formed.

"Luna," I whisper.

The shopkeeper is standing in front of me, so close. Too close, I think. If I wanted to, I could touch her.

"It's not safe out here," I warn her.

Her stark black hair blows in a breeze I do not feel. It flutters off her chest, revealing the crescent moon necklace I have seen before. The silver glistens, a shining glow moving back and forth, from moon tip to moon tip. The longer I stare at it, the more mesmerizing it becomes.

"Let me go with you," she says. "I can help."

She offers me her hand, her nails short and painted black, but when I grab on to her, her grip tightens, her fingers lengthen, becoming thick and dark, warm and fleshy, long and wispy.

"*You*," I hiss.

The man, the monster, he thought he could trick me, but this time, I won't let him win. I understand his game, and I have come to play.

I lunge forward, and he smiles at me tauntingly. I strike outward, sawing away at his flesh with my nails. I only stop when her screams overpower my own.

The man laughs as he fades away, and everything becomes clearer. The monster is no longer in front of me, but the shopkeeper is there. I watch as Luna falls, the softness of her smooth, pale skin turning lifeless as she crumbles to a heap at my feet.

Her body is angled awkwardly. Her legs are tucked and broken. Her arms are resting beside her, one reaching for me. Long, deep gashes decorate her torso, and I know the blood on my hands is hers.

Her face is pleading, but her eyes, wide and soulless, are vacant.

I stare at Luna, processing what just happened, what I just did.

You killed her . . .

The words circle my mind, but I don't know who spoke them—the monster or me.

My chest heaves, and I struggle to breathe. I hold out my hands, staring at my blood-soaked fingers. Chunks of flesh and cloth are caked beneath my nails, and I scream.

You killed her, the monster repeats.

"You tricked me!" I shout.

I stop breathing, holding the breath in my lungs to avoid inhaling the scent of death. It's everywhere. I smell it, I see it, I feel it. I am soaked in it. I am sitting in its pool, bathing in blood.

"I killed her," I choke out.

I killed an innocent.

You killed her, and you liked it.

My heart leaps as his words loop in my mind. I am disgusted by the sight, by the vision of Luna's dead body at my fingertips, but even as a slop of bile threatens its way into my mouth, a cunning smile worms its way onto my face.

I fear he is right. I did kill an innocent, but did I like it?

I jolt awake, startling Jasik from his slumber. Heart pounding, chest heaving, I gasp for breath as I sit upright and dangle my legs off the side of the bed. Convulsing so bad the bed jiggles, I run a hand through my wet and sticky hair.

"Ava?" Jasik says cautiously. He reaches forward, resting his hand on my arm. "You're shaking."

My breathing becomes rapid, loud and exasperated, as I struggle to control myself. Tears threaten to spill, burning my eyes as I deny their exit.

The sight of Luna, the death of the little girl, they are all I can see. Even here, in the safety of my bedroom, I feel their presence, like their astral or ghost selves are haunting me now. They seek vengeance against me, against what I have done to them.

Sitting on the edge of the bed, I clutch my chest, gripping the sides of my arms. The amulet is there, burning like fire against my skin. And it is buzzing, loud and strong, yet another melody heard only by me.

Jasik crawls beside me, the mattress shifting as he slides close. He wraps an arm around my waist and pulls me toward him. I rest my full weight against his strength.

"What is happening to me?" I whisper, voice pained.

Jasik rubs my arm with one hand and holds me tightly with the other. He rests his chin atop my head and ruffles my hair with his nose as he breathes. It's so simple, the way he holds me, but being this close, knowing he is here to watch me break, makes me feel stronger.

"I don't know," he says softly, and he kisses my crown, the connection of his lips against my hair sending tingles shooting through my body from head to toe.

"I feel like I'm going crazy," I confess. "I can't control it, and I can't stop it."

"I know," he whispers. "We're going to help you."

"Do you promise?" I ask, voice breaking. "Promise you won't just leave?"

He pulls away abruptly, taking no time to consider the impact of his words, and he angles my head so my gaze meets his. His thumb rests against the small divot of my jaw, pressing firmly against bone. My skin prickles where he touches me, and I can feel my cheeks flush. His scent of mint and blood consumes me as I inhale every breath he exhales. He is so close our lips nearly touch.

"I will never leave you, Ava," he says, crimson eyes soft and hurt. "I promised you an eternity of health and happiness. Nothing will stop me from giving that to you."

My reflection betrays nothing. My eyes are still bright and crimson; the area closest to my pupil still swirls with the magic contained within. My skin is milky, pale, and smooth, yet it is still scarred from my many battles pre-vampirism. My hair is vibrant, a deep, dark brown that appears black to the untrained eye. I am still small but muscular. Everything about me remains the same. I even wear the same clothes.

These moments of normality are punctuated by something ominous. I may look the same on the outside, but inside, the acrid ruins of my soul cry out to me helplessly. By the time I hear my inner turmoil, the sound is smothered by something far more sinister. The darkness is veiled by shadows, protected by my inner gloom.

It is consuming my magic, stealing it bit by bit. A hybrid without magic is merely a vampire, but I am certain this particular evil has no intention of stopping at just my magic. It will eat away at everything I am, everything I stand for, until only it remains. Already, I am becoming an empty shell, steadily losing this battle.

I am aware of my descent, but its hold on me grows stronger every day. There are moments I think I can fight it, beat it at its own vindictive game of cat and mouse, but those thoughts are quickly silenced. I am within its clutches now, and I fear I may never be free.

When I exit my bedroom, hours have passed since I was jolted awake by my nightmares. Jasik has long since left me to my thoughts, a cruel punishment in the name of benevolence. After last night, he deemed it necessary for me to rest, a kind gesture at its core, but the silence shrouds my sanity in something foul. My sire believes clarity comes with peace, but peace only brings darkness.

As I near the stairs to descend to the first floor, I hear muffled voices. The sound, hushed and deliberate, slows my pace. They grow louder with each step. I work tirelessly to remain unheard and unseen, taking soft, intentional steps.

The doors to the bedrooms are all closed, the hallway silent, but I feel a presence beside me. I glance over my shoulder. No one is there. My eyes tell me I am alone, but my mind knows better. Too many times I have believed I was the hunter when I was the hunted.

I spin in circles, round and round, until I become dizzy. With each rotation, I find no one—no haunting spirit, no lingering vampire, no creeping hunter, no vengeful witch, no mysterious dreamwalker ... Nothing. No one. In this labyrinth of halls, I am alone, and even though my eyes are convinced, internally, I continue to tell myself someone is there. My skin prickles, the tiny hairs alerting me to a presence no one can see.

While I scan the hall, gaze lingering on each and every door, time continues moving forward. I am completely aware that my grasp on sanity and reality is slipping. But I am also aware I can do nothing to stop it.

The whisper-soft voices from downstairs are growing louder, catching my attention. I am grateful for even a moment of relief. My mind is still buzzing, looping unrealistic scenarios of what may be lurking behind the closed doors, but I am walking away, attention on the argument echoing through these walls.

The closer I walk toward the sound, the heavier the amulet becomes. Weighty against my skin, it begins to burn, sizzling my newly healed flesh. I wince, hissing through my clenched jaw. I scratch at the skin there, trying desperately to remain focused on what is being said. Even though I can't make out their words, I know they are speaking about me.

I sit on the top step, grasping the railing and leaning forward quietly. When I do this, I am able to peer downstairs unnoticed.

Jasik, Malik, Holland, and the witch are standing in the sitting room at the landing of the stairs. The doors to the conservatory are open, and light spills into the room, illuminating my friends' features in malevolent shades of gray. My amulet reacts, but inside, I squirm at the sight. Why am I the only one who doesn't trust her?

Speaking softly, my friends are silenced when the front door is thrust open. Wind rushes into the room, sending shivers down my spine. The assault of stagnant air becoming more lively puts me on edge. My senses are crazed, each trying to overpower the next.

The door is slammed shut, and Hikari and Jeremiah walk in. I grip the railing tighter, trying to steady my erratic breathing. I take long, slow breaths, but with each inhalation, I am reminded of the mortal in our midst. I narrow my gaze at Sofía, who, like the others, seems oblivious to my presence.

"We may have a problem," Hikari says.

"What happened?" Malik asks.

"Rogues?" Jasik adds quickly.

Jeremiah shakes his head. "There was an attack."

"But not by rogues?" Jasik clarifies.

"No, by wolves," Hikari says.

I freeze, and visions of my friends battling beasts like the one from my dreams haunt me. I avert my gaze from Sofía to Hikari, mentally assessing possible damage done.

Skin smooth, clothes fresh, hair shiny and spiky, Hikari appears unharmed, but her heart is racing. Her attention is on Jeremiah, who seems just as perplexed. A wolf attack in Darkhaven isn't exactly common, though it isn't unheard of. After all, the town is surrounded by forest, seemingly endless land covered in trees.

"Really? A wolf attack?" Holland asks.

Jeremiah glides to his lover's side, and they stand together, Holland leaning against Jeremiah for support. They're holding hands, and it makes my heart burst. It feels like decades have passed since I experienced physical interaction, like love and lust, trust and strength. I crave it now more than ever before.

"How did this happen?" Malik asks, voice hard as he crosses his arms over his chest.

"Who was the victim?" Jasik asks. He offers his older brother a pointed look. Malik seems to understand the silent message, because his features soften.

"I don't know who he is," Hikari says.

"Human?" Malik asks.

Jeremiah nods but doesn't speak. Standing beside Holland, he towers over his lover's much shorter frame.

"They are still looking into the fire," Hikari says. "The man was investigating the woods behind the witches' house. Apparently, tracks led him there."

Her gaze darts to Jasik, who remains emotionless. He doesn't confirm or deny that we have been there recently, which I appreciate. His silence will allow me to confess on my own terms.

"And he was attacked by a wolf?" Sofía asks. "Does that happen a lot around here?"

Hikari shrugs. "I suppose. We're surrounded by forest."

"I care more about the investigation," Malik says. "Why are they still looking into the fire?"

He is desperate to remain poised, but his eyes betray his concern. Humans investigating the fire may lead them to me, and I will lead them to my nestmates. I used to believe we could coexist, but now I'm not so sure. If the witches taught me nothing else, they showed me mortals fear what they do not understand—and that fear only leads to chaos.

"Maybe because people keep visiting the crime scene," Hikari says, brow arched. Again, her gaze is fixed on Jasik. Anger begins to boil in my gut, but I suppress it. I understand her frustration, even if it sets me on edge.

Turning toward his brother, Malik asks, "How many times have you visited the house?"

"Just a few times, but I won't be going back," Jasik says.

"And what about Ava?" Malik asks.

"She understands the risks involved," Jasik says.

"What exactly does that mean?" Hikari asks.

"Be direct," Malik orders, voice unmistakable.

"She and I have visited the property several times since the fire," Jasik says. "We've discussed the dangers, and I do believe she has no interest in returning."

I lean forward, hoping to get a better view. Jasik's admission has left me feeling anxious, and I am desperate to see their faces as my sire confirms their suspicions. But as I move closer, the steps creak under my weight.

The vampires freeze, all eyes on me. I know I am not hidden well enough not to be seen, so pretending I haven't just been caught eavesdropping, I decide to descend, palm gracing the railing as the others watch me enter their secret meeting space.

Jasik smiles at me, eyes bright and warm, but the others offer cold, hard gazes. They are cautious around me, and even though that truth upsets me, I don't blame them. Like humans, vampires fear what they don't comprehend, and there is nothing more startling than the power dripping from my fingertips.

I walk to Jasik's side, finding the warmth radiating from him comforting. Of course, it's not physical warmth he offers me—after all, he is a vampire. But something about his presence, his innate strength and undying devotion to our bond, gives me comfort. When he's around, the air shifts. It becomes balmy and soft and pure, but a single swipe of his fingertips against my skin sends my innards into a frenzy. From tepid to scorching, innocent to sensual, with nearly no time passing at all. I hope it's always like this, no matter what happens.

"How are you feeling today, Ava?" Malik asks, and I groan internally, eyes rolling.

"Honestly?" I ask, crossing my arms.

"That would be a nice change of pace," Hikari says pointedly.

Ignoring her, I say, "I'm tired of being asked how I am. Because *I am fine.*"

Malik nods slowly, gaze scanning the length of my

frame. He doesn't believe me. None of them do. I suppose they shouldn't, because while my soul retches, determined to spill every ounce of pain lingering within my shell, my mouth remains silent, my emotions suppressed by the darkness inside.

"I'm glad to hear that," Malik says, but forever guarded, he never softens to me.

I wonder if the trust we built will remain shattered long after I expose the truth about Sofía. Perhaps this is our new norm—him questioning, me dodging, the others growing more annoyed with each passing second.

"So what's going on?" I ask.

"There has been a wolf attack in the woods behind your mother's house," Malik says. "Do you know anything about that?"

"Why would I know anything about that?" I ask plainly. "I've been here."

"You were gone last night," he counters. "You were away from the manor for several hours."

"I patrolled, and I didn't see any wolves," I say, answering his question before he even asks it.

"Did you visit the house?" he asks.

"I did," I say, opting for honesty.

He sighs sharply before speaking. "But you saw nothing?"

"I said I didn't see anything. How many times do I have to tell you that? I know nothing about the wolves, and I know nothing about Jackson Griggs. I didn't see the attack, and I would rather not answer the same three questions over and over again."

The room falls silent, all eyes on me. The grandfather clock in the upstairs hallway echoes loudly, and with each tick, the quiet begins to envelop the room.

I am reminded of how much I hate lying. I'm not particularly good at it, yet I continue to keep secrets. I remind myself that my nestmates gave me no other choice. By trusting *her*, they ousted *me*.

"You said you know nothing about Jackson Griggs, yet you know his name," Malik says. "You met him, didn't you? You *talked* to him, didn't you? Even after I specifically warned you about the dangers, you still went back."

Malik's voice grows deeper and louder with every accusation he throws at me. The verbal lashing leaves me weak at the knees, but I refuse to crumble under his downward gaze. I am especially certain I will not break in front of *her*.

"Leave the room," he orders, and I know he is not speaking to me. The others clear out. Only Jasik remains.

"Do you understand how dangerous this is?" Malik asks. "You risk every neck in this house when you disobey my rules."

"Relax," I say, but I only anger him further. "I didn't even speak to him."

"Tell me *everything*," he orders.

"Yes, I went to the house after patrolling, and I saw him. But he never saw me. His back was to me the whole time. I haven't even seen his face."

"Then how do you know his name?" Malik asks.

"He was speaking to another witch. She didn't like him either," I add. "That's when I learned his name."

"What else do you know?" Jasik asks, his voice calm and soothing.

"Not much," I admit. "He moved here from the city. He has a younger brother. His parents are dead." I shrug.

"He's investigating the fire?" Malik asks.

I nod.

"Do you understand *why* it is important that you never return?" Malik asks. "You can't be seen, Ava. Ever. Not until everyone who knows you has long since passed away. When you're finally allowed to travel, there can be no living connection to your mortal life. Do you understand what I am saying? Do you understand how important it is that you not be seen?"

"Why do you think I stayed in the shadows?" I ask. I don't bother to hide my annoyance. "He *didn't* see me."

"The humans *must* believe you died in the fire," Malik says. "That is the only way to ensure your safety. By going to town, you put us all at risk. If they think you are still alive, they will not stop until they find you. You are seventeen, Ava. You're still a child."

I scoff. "I am *not* a child."

"You certainly act like one," Malik says. "And if you continue to do so, you will leave me with no choice but to expel you from this house."

I gasp, stunned by his words. After everything that has happened, after all our fights and my continued disobedience, I expected him to threaten expulsion from the nest, but hearing it aloud still hurt. It feels like I'm back at home, with my mother, listening as she tells me to pack my bags before the coven unleashes their magic upon me. There is never compromise. It's either their way or death.

Malik sighs heavily. "Ava, I am a leader now. The survival of this nest relies on the decisions I make. The others count on my protection. With Amicia gone ... " He shakes his head, trailing off.

My heart sinks when Malik speaks her name. I realize I

haven't thought much about Will or Amicia in several days. I have been consumed by my hatred for Sofía, allowing that to take priority over even the safety of my friends. The realization guts me. Malik is right. I have been acting like a child. My anger erupts so quickly now; I don't always see it coming, but I certainly feel its aftermath.

"I know you don't want to hear this," Malik says, "but that amulet *is* affecting you. You must destroy it."

I grab it, clasping the stone in my palm. It scratches against my skin, warm and rigid. As much as I hate its influence, as much as I feel it chipping away at my sanity, everything inside me is screaming to protect it, to shield it from the others. I understand that it is controlling me in every way my friends fear, but my realization isn't enough to overpower it.

The anger I felt earlier returns, threatening to spill over, to seep from my lips in the form of words I can never take back. A dark spell is at my fingertips, one that will ensure allegiance. The thought of hexing the vampires makes the darkness inside rumble with delight.

But too focused on Malik's words, I don't chant my curse. My supposed allies are turning against me, all siding with the witch we barely know. Why is it I am the only one who sees her for who she truly is? A con artist. A drifter with means and opportunity to secure the most powerful amulet ever in existence. She wants what I have, and I refuse to relinquish it willingly.

"Sofía has offered to stay and help Holland develop a ritual that will be strong enough to destroy the amulet," Malik continues. He speaks softly, trying his very best to calm my nerves, but it doesn't work. He only infuriates me more.

"Are you serious? How has she blinded you to the truth?"

I ask, scoffing at his suggestion. "You can't possibly believe I would accept any form of help from *her*."

"Ava, you're being ridiculous," Malik says. "She has had plenty of opportunities to harm us, and she hasn't. Even you can admit that's very telling of her motivations. Clearly, she is here on friendly terms."

"Maybe she's buying your loyalty with false promises, simply biding time until the moment is perfect. A failed attempt at eliminating this nest will result in her death. She knows that. She can't strike until the moment is right. *That* is something you should know well. Isn't it your job to train the newbies? To teach us how to battle and be vampires and *survive*?"

Malik exhales sharply. "I wish you could hear yourself. You sound . . . " He shakes his head, scratching at his buzzed scalp.

"Crazy? You think I'm *crazy*?" I ask, voice squeaky. "Do you know what is crazy? The fact that no one else finds it even *slightly* peculiar that Sofía arrived in Darkhaven at the same time as the rogue who nearly killed us all. And it just so happens that a new investigator is in town too. I find it *crazy* that a small town like Darkhaven gets a population boost in a matter of days, and no one else thinks that's suspicious."

"Ava," Sofía says.

I turn to face her, finding them all there. My nestmates are watching me, and though they never speak, their silence speaks volumes. Even Jasik stands beside them. He is my quiet, reserved, and ever-faithful sire whose bond to me seems to be weakening. Only moments ago, I praised him for his devotion, but when I look at him now as he stands beside them and not me, I am forced to question his loyalty.

Sofía walks over, offering her best smile, her most

empathetic eyes. With soft features and arms extending to me questioningly, nothing about her demeanor is threatening, and that only ignites my anger more.

"I promise, I just want to help you," Sofía says. "I want to help before it's too late."

Still clutching the amulet, I release it, and the room erupts in gasps. I feel it against my skin, burning brightly, and I hear it all around me, buzzing loudly. I don't need to question that the others sense it too. I know they do. Finally, the amulet is making them aware of its power, of its strength.

"I will never destroy the amulet," I say, but I hardly recognize my voice. Dark and gritty, wicked and spiteful, the darkness speaks from within.

FIVE

The air is unkind tonight. It assaults my senses, a steady stream of erratic temperatures and salty sea breezes. Spring is upon us now, and the abrupt change of seasons leaves me on edge.

After my confrontation with Sofía, I decided to distance myself from the others. I stand outside, far away from their unruly gazes.

They want my amulet. When they speak, they warn me about its uncontrollable power and deem what is best for me, for my safety. But it is what is said between sentences that matters most. Their silence is profound, and I am noticing an undeniable truth.

They want the black onyx crystal. They want its power to harness as their own, but I will never relinquish it.

This truth makes the darkness happy, and I am overwhelmed by a sudden warmth. It calms my shivers, easing my anxiousness. My anger subsides, and the entity within grants me a moment of peace. I savor these moments, when the world falls silent and all I can hear is the whispering from within the stone.

"I will keep you safe," I respond as I stroke the rough edges of the crystal. It is harsh against the pad of my thumb, but I like it. It reminds me that it's there.

"Ava?" someone says from behind me. I spin on my heels, meeting Jasik's unreadable gaze. His brows are furrowed, eyes narrowed, as he stares down at me, his height towering over my small frame.

In this light, I see all the little things I missed inside the manor. His hair is disheveled, messy and dry, and his eyes are sunken, their usual cool crimson color muddled and dim. Beneath his eyes there are dark circles, and I wonder how long he hasn't been sleeping.

His frame is lanky, his chiseled chin appearing bonier, his jawline sharp. All his features are more defined, as though he hasn't fed in weeks. I had no idea his concern for my well-being has been affecting him so drastically.

I reach for him, letting my fingertips linger against his soft skin. He rests his cheek against my palm and closes his eyes as he smiles. I feel the weight of him against me, the vulnerability and trust, and it silences the darkness. I discover true peace lies only with him.

"Jasik," I whisper, and he opens his eyes to meet my gaze.

"Will you come back inside?" he asks.

"I need space," I say, knowing he will understand. "I'm going to patrol, clear my head a bit."

He nods, breaking my gaze to scan our surroundings. I lower my arm so I can turn away from him.

The woods are dark tonight, the clouds covering what little light we need to hunt. The trees sway in the wind, their shadows lunging forward like monsters in the dark. These shadow figures lash out at my nerves, and my anxiety intensifies.

"Will you be going back?" my sire asks.

"Back where?" I ask. I cross my arms over my chest,

rubbing my bony palms against the fabric of my jacket. A shudder creeps its way down my spine.

"To the house," he says.

I shake my head. "There is nothing for me there."

He is quiet for a moment as he processes my confession. It isn't a lie. My parents are dead, my home reduced to ash. My coven perished, my belongings scorched. All that awaits me in that place are painful memories—ones I don't care to relive. His earlier promise to Malik was not a lie. I won't be going back. Ever.

"Please come back inside," he says, voice breaking.

"I'm not ready yet," I admit.

I consider mentioning Sofía, but I know there is no use. He knows my feelings—they all do. And they still trust her. They know I never will. Until I provide solid proof that she is up to no good, I don't stand a chance in turning them against her. It shouldn't be that way. They are *my* friends, not hers, but they don't trust me anymore. The amulet may hang around my neck, but the weight of its strength and power is over their heads. Until I destroy the stone, they will not side with me.

I descend the front porch steps, tossing a glance over my shoulder when I reach the center garden. The grass is still dead from the long, cold winter months, but life is slowly emerging. Vibrant flowers are scattered around the yard, confirming the seasonal shift. The flowers are short and invasive, covering the earth in an indigo blanket. In a few weeks, they'll be gone, covered by something new. Evidence of their time here will be ripped away with the first mow or trampling feet or by something new that grows in its place, and just like everything else I used to love, these flowers will live only in my memory.

I reach down and pick one, plucking each purple petal

as I turn back and stare at the manor. Everything I cherish is inside—friends who have become family, what little belongings I managed to save—but I am outside, left to gawk at the place that was meant to be a fresh start, a new home. I was supposed to make good memories, not enemies.

I teeter as I stand on the cobblestone pathway that leads to the house, a timeless Victorian manor that stands three stories tall. Among the trees, the sight is jarring. With startling overhangs, sharp edges, and stained-glass windows, the house doesn't belong here. No other home in Darkhaven mirrors its construction. Like me, it's an outcast, extraordinary among the ordinary.

At the top of the stairs to the wraparound front porch, I spot the stone gargoyle. I stare at him, wondering when was the last time I acknowledged him as I passed. The greeting became tradition, a ritual I was certain I could not shake. But I can't remember when I last spoke to him. I glance at the palm of my hand. It looks the same as it always has, but the feeling is there. I am shamed by my actions, pained by what I've done. The list of my forgotten loves is growing—first Will and Amicia, now the unnamed gargoyle. Who will be next?

Jasik is still on the porch, standing in front of the French-style double doors. His jeans and black shirt blend into the dark wood and gray stained-glass windows, but his skin, pale white, glows in the sleek streams of moonlight that break through the hovering clouds. He looks at me, eyes heavy with uncertainty, with longing. The longer I stare at him, the more I notice something else in his gaze: fear. Like the others, he is scared, but I can't distinguish if he is scared *for* me or *of* me.

I step back, growing the distance between us. When I bump into the black wrought-iron fence that encloses the property, I stop. The rooftop comes to several points, all abrupt in composition. At the very tip, the front focal point, there is a subtle yet striking weather vane. At its tip there is a prominent spear, a death dagger that nearly pierces the sky.

I blink, and my imagination takes hold. I envision the many battles fought on this land, and at the very top of the house, I see the victims piled high, guts punctuated by the spear. Blood cascades down the roof, seeping into the manor's very foundation. The property is impressive without the crimson wave, but with it, the sight steals my breath. This vision mimics my dream, in which Darkhaven was flooded by the blood of the innocent.

I squeeze my eyes shut, chest heaving, heart racing, as I try to steal back my sanity. I tell myself it's not real; it's only my imagination playing with my emotions, which are running high and uncontrollable these days.

But this does not work. My knees wobble, and I become unsteady on my feet. I turn away from the house, from the vision of death and despair, and I face the woods. I grab on to the iron daggers, wrapping my hands around the small points of the crosses topping each metal rod in the fence.

What once gave me strength melts my skin. I clench my jaw and yank my hands away. The stabbing pain at my palms worms its way through my arms, and I stare at my hands in disbelief. Brand marks in the form of perfect crosses are etched into my skin, and the amulet buzzes and burns against my chest. I groan, snarling as I slowly begin to heal from dual attacks.

Likely noticing my distress, Jasik is behind me now, eliminating the space I put between us, and he rests his hands on my shoulders. I turn to face him, snuggling against his chest as the pain begins to lessen.

My sire holds me tightly, slithering his fingers through my hair and rubbing the tension from my scalp. I burrow into his chest, pushing so hard I am certain we will become one, morphing together until I'm not sure where he ends and I begin. But his sturdy frame never gives way to mine, even when he groans against my ferocity.

We are silent, both too scared to admit what this means. I can no longer touch the cross, a powerful relic from my days as a mortal. I can't rely on its strength, on its protection from rogue vampires. I am scared to ask Jasik why this is happening, because deep down, I already know the answer—and so does he.

Only one thing has changed since I transitioned into a vampire. I now carry the burden of protecting this amulet, the home of the entity summoned by the witches, and the evil within is seeping from its crystal shell and tainting me in darkness.

In moments like this, I think about taking off the amulet and storing it somewhere safe until it can be destroyed, but those ideas are quickly smothered, and the blanket used to extinguish that desire wraps around me tightly, squeezing so hard I can't breathe.

My chest aches with that pain, even now, even as I am fully aware of what is happening to me. Even though I know what will happen, I still think about removing the amulet and destroying the darkness, but as I do, from the obsidian depths within the crystal, evil grabs on to me, wrapping its fingers around my neck and muting my effort to find strength in my sire.

"The woods are beautiful this time of night," Jasik says.

My sire is walking beside me, scanning our surroundings. The moonlight is streaming through the clouds, illuminating the trees. Flowers are beginning to bloom, and even in the darkness I can see how they light up the world around us.

An early shower has left the forest sparkling with dew, the petals and leaves glistening like magic. The moisture coats the air, and we are surrounded by a dazzling haze.

He's right. The forest is glorious at night, but I am too distracted to appreciate the delicacy of new life, the subtle grace of rebirth after a long, cold winter.

The familiar sound of branches breaking halts our hike, the snap of an intruder silencing our deepest thoughts. At once, we are acutely aware that we are not alone in these woods.

Jasik is the first to move, stepping forward to scan the trees in the distance. Seldom do I feel fear—real, true, spine-tingling, gut-churning terror—but I am awash in anxiety now as I stare into the eyes of at least a half dozen rogue vampires.

Unlike my sire, I am frozen in time, still chastising myself for allowing other predators to sneak up on us so easily. My internal battle is moot, but even knowing this doesn't stop me from berating myself.

When I attempt to move forward, to meet Jasik stride by stride as he begins to close in on our intruders, he stops me with the raise of his arm, his hand a clear indicator that I am not to proceed.

I obey, even though every fiber of my being is itching for this fight. Taking my stress and frustration out on a willing participant may be just what I need to overcome my newfound turmoil. I see this as a blessing in disguise, a necessary attempt at clearing my conscience. I haven't been the greatest nestmate lately, and apparently, I need to restore my rank in this pack. What better way to prove my loyalty than by killing a half dozen rogues?

By the time they begin their approach, we realize too late that we have fallen into a trap—but a trap for whom? I find it unlikely this many rogues were hunting for dinner in the same spot. They are here for something—or *someone*—specific. Not for a quick, easy meal. For Jasik. Or for me.

The ground rumbles, the echoing vibration of a half dozen rogue vampires in hot pursuit of their end goal. The sensation worms its way up my legs, piercing my heart. It beats loud and steadily in my head, helping to drown out the soul-crushing sound of impending doom. I hoped a fight would ease my panic, but it's only getting worse. Regardless, we have a job to do, so we fall into mindless pursuit.

We spring into action, separating from each other to tackle the rogues closest to each of us. Focusing solely on my intended targets, I ignore the sounds of Jasik's battle cries as they waft over to me.

The first rogue splits from his friends, choosing to charge me full on. I have seen this maneuver countless times in battle, and it never ends well. I can thank Malik's training sessions for the ease of eliminating my first threat. When they make it this easy, I don't even bother summoning the elements.

He lunges forward, and I leap into the air at the last second, flipping over him and landing on my feet a few feet behind him. I spin, finding my target skidding to a stop. But I move too quickly for him.

I pounce before he has the chance to locate me and leap

onto his back, wrapping my arms around him. I secure one arm around his neck and the other across his torso. I squeeze and claw, digging my nails into his flesh with a ferocity seen only in animals, but it does the job. I slash through flesh, meeting bone. He combusts quickly, evaporating into dust. I end his life before he even realizes he's dead.

I fall to the ground but rise quickly, spinning to face the others. Two stand before me, gazes narrowed. The younger-looking rogue is much smaller than the other. He looks weak, like he was changed on his deathbed and never fully recovered from the transition. He is thin and lanky, only a few inches taller than me. By comparison, the rogue beside him is his true counterpart. He is tall and muscular, with a strong jawline and a scowl to match.

I set my sights on the stronger of the two. While I know eliminating the weaker of the two will be quick and easy work, I can't risk taking my eyes off the other one. Over my years of hunting in these woods, I've learned defeating the immediate threat is always the best first step to a successful patrol. The stronger of the two is the clear alpha here, and I plan to waste no time in showing him that I am the better fighter.

I rush forward, dashing from side to side to keep him on his toes, but he anticipates my attack, knowing I would leap at him first. He meets my chest with his fist and sends me soaring through the air, crashing into the base of a nearby tree. My sternum cracks at the impact of his hand against my bone, and I struggle to breathe, sucking in deep, loud gasps as I slide down the tree and land on the ground.

The air is heavy and wet, and with each inhalation, my lungs are coated. I hack and nearly faint from the surge of pain stabbing at my heart. The thought of a rib snapping and piercing the vital organ leaves me distracted.

The rogue is hovering over me, almost angelic-looking in the streams of moonlight. My vision blurs, dotted in spots as my mind blanks from the pain as my crushed bone begins to heal, and I almost believe the rogue is actually floating. Only after several seconds pass and my vision begins to clear do I understand that *I* am the one floating, held upright by the vampire's strong arms.

I stare into his lifeless crimson eyes as he grips my arms, squeezing so tightly I'm surprised my flesh hasn't given way to his strength. He is only inches from my body, and my gaze settles on the veins protruding from his neck as he overexerts himself. They decorate his skin in distinct lines that make my stomach grumble. If he hears my hunger, he does not acknowledge it.

I hiss as he tightens his grasp, and he jerks me forward and slams me back again, digging my spine into the sharp edges of the tree trunk. As my jacket rides up, the bark scrapes against exposed skin, and I grind my teeth at the sudden ache.

With my arms still pinned in place, hands dangling at my hips, the rogue does this again and again, tossing my body around like a rag doll. The back of my head makes contact with the tree trunk too many times to count, and I begin to see stars, falling limp in his embrace.

Fingers dig into my flesh, dirty nails piercing skin. Blood rushes down my arms, pooling on the ground. I hear the distinct splatters of my life soaking into the earth, seeping deep and out of reach. My legs dangle, and even with the tips of my toes pointed downward, I cannot reach the ground.

He holds me close and tight so I cannot move. My head

lolls from side to side, the bones in my spine cracking, slowly giving way to a superior force, and when I hear something crack deep within my abdomen, I shriek from the biting pain.

I hear the distant calls of someone shouting my name, but his voice is drifting away, muffled by the screeching cries within my own mind. His voice is soaked in anguish, stressed and pained, the words jolting me upright, and I blink away my blurred vision. As Jasik screams my name, he startles me back to reality.

The rogue is no longer pinning me against the tree. Likely believing I have submitted to his dominant strength, he has wrapped both hands around my neck. He believes I am too distracted, too weakened by his attack, to realize his intention, to stop his final attack. This will be his fatal flaw.

I thrust my fists upward, smacking my balled hands into the rogue's wrists, loosening his grip on me. His eyes widen as he stumbles backward, granting me only a couple feet of space. But it's enough for me to slam the center of my palm into his chest. He expels the air from his lungs in a haggard breath, and I bring my fist upward, meeting his jaw. The distinct, sloppy smack of his teeth closing on his tongue rattles my bones, and the rogue howls as blood spews from his mouth. A slimy, meaty chunk slaps against my jacket and falls to the ground between us.

I am coated in his excrements, face and body sprayed with spit and blood. I imagine I look like the final scene of a horror film when the sole survivor reveals she has thwarted every effort the killer threw at her. I may be drenched to the skin, but I have never felt more revitalized. I lick my lips and smile, garnering a look of shock and disgust from my victim.

My fist penetrates his sternum with ease. I break through

bone, finding nothing but soft, mushy flesh that pops and oozes when I squeeze it. The rogue combusts before me, and his ash coats my already uncomfortably wet skin.

When I turn to face the final rogue, something startling happens. We make eye contact, the smaller allowing his gaze to linger as he scans the length of my body, and when he finally settles again on my eyes, it clicks in his mind. He is going to die tonight. And I am going to kill him.

He turns and runs, fleeing in the opposite direction. If I weren't worried about allowing a rogue to go free, I would find it comical, but instead, I am annoyed. A high-speed chase on foot is the last thing I want to do.

For as sickly as he appeared to be, the final rogue certainly can run. I struggle to keep up as I leap over fallen brush and shimmy under low-hanging branches. On the other hand, he scours each mound with ease.

He glances back, watching as I close in, and before he turns away from me, he trips, flinging himself forward and rolling to a stop. I reach him as he stands, wrapping my arm around his neck and flinging his body backward. As he falls, I twist, snapping his head clean off.

I stand, dusting off my jacket that is now caked in ash, and wipe the blood from my face. It's wasted effort—only a good soak will wash away the grime.

Giving up, I scan the forest for Jasik, finding no sign of him. I close my eyes, listening for his location. I hear the distant echoes of his battle, but something else catches my attention.

I nearly choke on my breath as I turn, noticing several things at once. I am no longer in the middle of the forest, battling rogues to keep the village safe. I am at the edge of Darkhaven, close to Main Street and even closer to the humans I vowed to protect. More importantly, I am standing only several feet away from an onlooker, a witness who has just watched me kill a rogue vampire.

The girl gasps and takes several steps backward. She moves farther from me but closer to the nearby streetlights, which illuminate her appearance in an eerie glow. The breeze picks up, blowing the clouds to allow moonlight to shine down on us, and I cringe at the sight of her.

Because I know this human, and now, she knows me.

"Luna," I whisper softly.

The shopkeeper, the happy girl who sold me a book without ever realizing I'm not human, is now completely aware of the existence of vampires. I have broken the golden rule, the only one all magical beings actually agree on: never, *ever* expose our secret to mortals.

Malik will deem this unforgivable.

She must be silenced.

The thought comes quickly, resonating from the dark craters of the amulet to the deep depths of my soul. The voice in my head, speaking confidently and loudly, is not my own, but I believe it. I understand the intention, the meaning behind this thought.

Luna has to die.

I think she understands it too, perhaps she even hears the voice. Maybe my features shift, my face contorting into something malevolent. Maybe I appear as I truly am: a monster. Or maybe she senses my decision like I smell her fear. I inhale deeply, smiling. She smells like honey and lavender and *blood*.

I don't know *how* she knows my inner thoughts, but it is clear she hears them. Like the rogue, Luna is aware that she will die tonight. And I will kill her, just as I killed them. This pleases the black onyx crystal, and it rewards me with a warm, soft buzz at my chest. It remained silent for my previous battles, but now, at the very moment I must take a mortal life, it springs awake, relishing in my damned, dark deeds.

She takes another step back, almost tripping over her feet. She catches herself, correcting her fall so she remains upright, but in doing so, she looks away. She glances back, tossing a careless look over her shoulder to steady her footing. By the time she straightens and refocuses her attention on me, I am no longer standing at the same spot.

She shrieks as we make eye contact. I am close now; only a foot or so separates our bodies. I grab her by the throat, squeezing just enough to silence her scream.

She is already crying, the sounds escaping her mouth muffled and weak. Steady streams of tears coat my hand, dripping down my arm. Her heart is beating strong and fast, the sound morphing into a melody in my mind. It makes my own heart sing. I smile at the music that only I can hear.

I wonder if I look different to her. Is she remembering my visit to her shop? Is she finally noting all the weird moments that she missed, like how I avoided her and kept my distance, how I never looked her in the eyes, how I tossed some bills on the counter and walked out with the book, not waiting for change? Did she notice then how pale I am, how strong I look, how good I smell?

As a predator, I have innate qualities that welcome her to me, that make her want to come closer. This is how we survive, even though immortals are severely outnumbered—this is how we will rise.

"Please," she whispers, nearly choking on the word. The lenses of her teal-framed glasses are smudged and streaked with lines by her eyelashes. Her gray eyes are muddled and watery.

Her request for mercy will be denied. I can't risk her exposing the truth about our existence. One life must be lost in order to prevent an entire species from annihilation. Even though I understand this, I am sorry it has to be her, and that makes me pause. I barely know this girl, yet I care for and desire her in strange ways. She should be no one to me.

I break eye contact by glancing down at her neck. Her skin is bright and light, and I can see strips of it between the spaces of my fingers. Even in this darkness, her milky complexion is almost more than I can handle. I *ache* for her, to feed, to taste, to relish just one time.

Visions of my nightmares reel through my mind. I remember killing her in my dreams, tasting her blood. For a moment, I envision I am rogue, soulless and careless, living only for my current needs. The freedom, the power...

I step closer, body shaking, nerves jittery. It is almost impossible to hold back. Luna's hair is hanging at her shoulders, jet black and shiny, and her fringe is poking past her glasses, now streamed by her tears.

I run my hand through her locks, tangling my fingers in the thick tresses. I fist a bundle of her hair right at her scalp, and I release her neck. I tug, pulling her head back and angling it so I can better see the protruding vein in her neck.

She whimpers but never screams. I admire her strength, her courage, and I wonder if that confidence makes the blood taste sweeter.

My fangs are throbbing, the excitement building within. I suck in a sharp breath, and it makes a hissing noise between my teeth. I want to tell her how much I will enjoy this, but instead, I tell her it will only hurt for a second.

Then she'll be dead. The pain will be gone. This should make her happy, but tears still flow.

Take her, the voice says, and I oblige.

I yank her toward me, and her body crashes against mine. We are almost the same height, and her soft curves collide with my more solid frame. I am sturdy and strong, whereas she is supple and weak. She will make an excellent first feed.

My mouth is at her neck, but before I indulge, I grant myself one last pleasure. I inhale slowly, deeply, until my lungs ache from expansion. There is a stabbing pain, but I don't want to stop breathing. I want to remember her scent, imprint it in my memory, forever. That is the only way a mortal truly lives on—within the memory of a vampire.

My fangs pierce her skin, and I lick the dribble of blood that seeps from her wounds. It is everything I hoped it would be: thick and savory yet sweet and tart at the same time. My taste buds explode from the flavor, and I understand why so many vampires go rogue. A blood bag will never taste the same. Not after tonight.

Luna screams and scratches at me, exerting everything she has to push me away, but I never budge. She doesn't have the strength to save herself, not against a vampire and certainly not against a hybrid on the verge of tempting darkness.

Yet my grip on her is loosening. Space separates us as she is ripped away from my grasp. I open my eyes to find her stumbling backward, tumbling to the ground and sliding across the sidewalk. She is several yards away now.

I growl, a hearty bellow erupting from my chest, and I am engulfed in my anger. Her blood, rich and smooth, creamy and bursting with flavor, has been torn away, leaving me empty and hungry, irritable and rash.

Jasik is beside me, his grasp on me tighter than any embrace I have ever experienced, especially from him. His features are hard, his eyes emotionless. He holds only one arm, so I use the other as a means of escape.

I raise my arm to force him away, but he is older, wiser, *faster*. He catches my balled fist, covering my hand with his own. He squeezes so hard, bones snap, and I gasp at the stabbing pain. Immediately, I begin to heal, but my hesitance is all he needs.

He yells for me to control myself, to stop this, but I ignore him. Nothing matters to me but Luna's blood. The scent is still too strong, coating everything around us in a fine mist. I still hear her heart, and it is pounding now, threatening to burst. *I* want to be the one who is showered in her blood when that happens.

"I don't want to hurt you, Ava," Jasik says.

I believe him, but I also hear something else. A promise. A guarantee that he *will* hurt me if that is what he must do. Just like the others, when it comes down to it, his loyalty is *not* with me.

The amulet at my chest is hot and angry, fueling my own frustration. Jasik makes the mistake of glancing down, gaze focused on the stone as he frowns, and I make my move.

I lower my arms, pulling him closer to me, and I slam my forehead against his chin so hard it makes my brain ache. He stumbles back, hand covering the wound, but he never releases his grasp. Blood gushes through his fingers and splatters down his chest.

"You'll have to do better than that," he says through gritted teeth.

But before I can react, making good on that thought, he has me spinning, twirling 'round, a sharp pain shooting through my arm as he maneuvers too quickly for me to keep up. With my back to him, he pulls me close. He keeps his arms around me, pinning me against his much larger, much stronger body.

"Remember who you are," he whispers into my ear, breath cool against my skin. The blood pouring from his chin is slowing to a trickle, but some still splatters against my shoulder.

As his words loop in my mind, I allow the scent of my sire to coat my senses. It is familiar, a gentle mist that reminds me of home, of love and promise, of eternal life and the oath I took to keep the peace. I soften under him, as though tranced by merely the sound of his voice, the smell of his blood, the touch of his arm wrapped around my body. My sire speaks to me, soothing my raging emotions with promises he can't possibly keep.

The heat from the amulet lessens, the fire extinguished. That internal voice is silenced, but the darkness lingers, angry to be once again caged.

I relax in his arms, but several moments pass before Jasik trusts me enough to release me. When he finally does, I twist until I am facing him.

Jasik stares at me, still unsure, but the pain of our encounter, of what I just did, is still there. His shirt is drenched, his chin gashed. His crimson eyes are watery and distant, swirling with both magic and uncertainty for our future.

Jasik breaks eye contact to glance behind me. He curses, and I don't have to look; I know the girl is gone. Taking her one chance at life while we were busy sparring for dominance, she ran. We can't risk chasing her farther into town, so she will remain a loose end—one I hope won't return to bite me in the ass.

"I didn't mean to hurt her," I confess.

Jasik glances down at me and offers a weak smile. He reaches for me, and I fight the urge to flinch. He tucks loose hair behind my ear. His touch is soft, uncertain, but it slowly soothes my anguish nonetheless.

"I'm sorry," I whisper.

"I know," he says.

"I swear, I didn't mean to hurt her."

"Ava..." He exhales loudly as he trails off, finding the right words. "You aren't the same. You must see that now."

I nod and lean against him, resting my head against his chest. He stiffens beneath my touch, but I pretend not to notice. Still, inside, the thought of my sire being uncomfortable around me makes my heart burn, my soul ache. The bond we share is weakening, the link loosening with every irredeemable decision I make.

"We can't trust the amulet, Ava," he says. "The others believe it is influencing you. Holland has been researching a way to destroy it."

"We can't destroy it," I say, the words spilling quicker than I can process them.

"We *must* destroy it," he counters.

Even though I know he is right, I fear what will happen when we try. The darkness is listening, always lurking, always ready to best our attempts at freeing my tethered soul.

And from that darkness, I am left with one final realization: if this evil is vanquished, I will die too.

SIX

We walk back in silence, Jasik maintaining several feet of distance between us. I catch him staring at me as we hike toward the manor, likely checking to make sure I haven't completely turned rogue.

It's true I craved Luna's blood, the feeling overpowering every rational thought I had, but I feel better now. My hunger has been muted, and we are in the clear. Except he doesn't see it that way. He views me on the brink of madness, one bad decision away from ruining the life we have built together.

The closer we get to the manor, the worse I feel. The dread of Malik discovering what I did is weighing on me, and I know our leader won't take the news well. I think this is it. This is what will push him over the edge and condemn me to an eternity alone. The worst part is that I have no one to blame but myself.

I kick at the ground, sending a shower of decayed brush billowing forward. I sense Jasik's discomfort at my frustration, but I don't summon the courage to talk about what happened when I attacked the girl. I just hope he knows I'm mad at myself, not at him. I thought I had complete control over my blood lust, but clearly, I don't.

I think about Luna, about how she must be feeling right now. I imagine she is terrified to leave her house, believing the stories Hollywood tells humans about vampires. She probably thinks she is safe inside her house, the door securely closed and me without an invitation to enter. If only that actually made a difference. If I wanted to harm her, a piece of wood and the lack of an invitation wouldn't stop me. There's nothing she could do to stop me.

The thought of what I did to her flashes in my mind, and a small part of me enjoys reliving that moment. I am ashamed to admit the way her blood made me feel, how the way she cowered and crumbled beneath my grasp made the hunt that much more exciting for me. The surge of power was euphoric; I cling to the effects of our encounter. There was an unspoken agreement between us. She is prey and I am predator. She dies. I live. I still feel the tingle of her blood that pools in my stomach, her life force carving its way through my veins, ensuring my survival and her demise. I'm happy she was my first.

At that thought, the amulet warms against my skin. It remains silent, never alerting Jasik as it awakens to my darkest impulses. I love the way it reacts to me, the way it encourages me to live out my desires. Unlike the others, it understands me. I am immortal now, the creature at the very top of the food chain, and sometimes I just want to be bad.

Happily concentrated on my first taste of human blood straight from the tap, I am too distracted to notice the subtle change in the air, the way it shifts when it blows against my body. There is an absence in it, a noticeable difference in the way it caresses my skin. By the time I recognize the familiar sensation—the way my body alerts me to an onlooker, from hairs standing on end to the prickle down my spine—they are already revealing themselves to us.

Jasik must have missed them too, probably too distracted by practicing the rehearsed monologue in his mind—the one that tells me how wrong I was, how right they are—because he halts at the same moment I do. He clenches his jaw, his hands balled into fists at his sides. More than anything, he looks annoyed. The last thing he wants is for another battle to test my control.

There are at least a dozen of them. They step from the shadows in unison, moving as one solid unit. They stand in a crescent-shaped half circle, separating us from our destination. The manor looms in the distance, but it is too far away, the haze too thick; we can't see it from where we stand. But we know it is there, and inside, our friends are waiting, blissfully unaware of the chaos ensuing outside.

Crimson irises dot the night in an ominous glow. The moon is suddenly hiding behind the clouds, but the breeze is strong tonight. The clouds are moving swiftly across the sky, and they will soon unveil a truth we are not prepared to accept: we are severely outnumbered.

The rogue vampires stand before us and then begin their approach. They believe the fight will be quick, our demise effortless, but they are wrong. I have no intention of dying tonight.

Jasik and I stand side by side, and I grab his hand, linking our fingers together. Despite his earlier hesitance, he allows me this subtle comfort. Simply being near him strengthens me, steadies my racing heart.

Still exhausted from our earlier battle, I fear he and I aren't exactly prepared to fight what is certainly a losing effort. We are remarkably outnumbered and too far from friends to rely on help. Even if they hear our cries, by the time they make it to us, they would be too late. Instead of helping us rise, they would watch us fall.

I glance at Jasik, who remains cool and calm under what is undoubtedly intense stress. He is far too collected for my liking. His gaze remains focused on the approaching rogues, his jaw clenched, his body tense. He squeezes my hand hard, and I wonder if he remains stiff because that soothes his shaking nerves. What is he really worried about? My control or our survival?

Perhaps sensing my concern, he glances over at me and offers a forced smile. With it, he tells me we will be okay, even though we both know that is a lie. We can't fight our way out of this—at least not if we rely on our vampire abilities. We need something stronger, something faster, something the rogues can't stop with the smack of fists.

By nature, rogues are stronger. They survive on fresh human blood, which makes them more powerful, but we are smarter, driven by something far better than hunger. Our brains will always outmatch their muscle, and I am well aware that there is only one way I can save us.

Accessing magic is our only hope, but in order to harness enough power to eliminate every rogue here means weakening my resolve, lowering the walls I have built to protect myself from the evil within the amulet. To save us, I would have to risk my very soul. Jasik would never allow this. But I can either appease my sire and die, or I can summon magic and save us both. Does he really expect me to choose death over life?

As much as I would like to continue clinging to Jasik's hand, securing our connection as a single, unified front, I have to separate myself from him. Allowing our bodies to remain tethered is a distraction I cannot risk.

I pull away, slipping my hand free from his grasp. He releases me with hesitancy, and I ignore the look of concern that flashes behind his eyes. I step forward, and Jasik remains behind me. Somehow, I know that he knows exactly what I plan to do.

I tear my gaze away from my sire to focus on the rogue vampires, but before I can summon my magic, something slams into my body, and I am soaring through the air. I am stopped when I land on the ground, my legs jutting outward at an awkward angle. A stabbing pain shoots through my thigh, penetrating my spine.

I can still move, but the attack has slowed me considerably. Clawing at the ground, I struggle to get up. I notice someone is standing beside me, and it takes everything I have not to whimper beneath him. Only moments ago, I was the hunter. Now I am the hunted.

I stare at the unfamiliar set of dirty brown boots just as one makes contact with my face. I am flung backward, landing on my back. The sharp, jagged edge of a rock nestled in the dirt stabs at my spine, and I hiss, jutting upward and curving my back to alleviate the pain.

But my attacker is relentless. He assaults me again and again. Blood spews from my nose and soaks the ground where I cower for mercy. I am trembling, vision blurred as I withstand each vicious strike.

Just when I think I can't take another minute, that my very bones may shatter and turn to dust, it stops. He is crouched beside me, so close I can taste his scent. He smells like stale cigarettes and ash, like old blood and mildew. His putrid breath is nauseating, and I swallow down blood and bile. He is close to my ear, his sticky breath hot on my neck.

I turn away from him, plopping onto my stomach and staring at the ground. I gather a fistful of dirt as I dig my hands in the ground. My nails are caked in earth, and I notice it looks no different from the cremains of the many vampires I have killed.

I spit up bright-red blood, feeling it dribble down my chin. Unable to meet his gaze, I still haven't looked at him, my sight fixed on the pool of blood before me.

The rogue steps closer, eliminating the space I managed to give us, and he whispers to me, his voice low and raspy. There is an edge, anger in his tone, and I know even though we have never met, his hatred is for me.

"Make this easier on him and just stay down," he whispers, voice seething.

Slowly, I piece together what he means, who he is talking about, and when the realization strikes me, my blood runs cold. The abrupt certainty of his threat makes me light-headed, my vision blurring momentarily as I get my bearings.

I groan internally, jaw clenched, teeth grinding, as I struggle to push myself upright. Surprisingly, the rogue allows me to move, and I look past him, scanning the distance for Jasik. The remaining rogue vampires surround my sire, and I watch as he struggles to dodge their repeated, relentless attacks. Only one rogue is beside me. The others haven't even looked at us.

They came for him, for Jasik.

Jasik is struck in the back, stabbed by a thick, pointed stick. I hear the wet smack of his flesh as the rogues strike him again and again. My sire's cries echo deep within my soul. I feel his pain just as he does, as though our bond links us not just in life but in death too. Is this how he felt when Amicia died? The sense of urgency to protect him, to take his place in death, is overwhelming.

His knees buckle, and he slams to the ground, the vibration resonating within my own legs. I am shaking so hard I can't tell if I am moving because it pains me to see my sire wounded or if the physical manifestation of his attack truly is so powerful it is shaking the ground we walk on.

He is struck again, and this time, the sloppy bellow escaping his lips is wet with blood.

I scream, the sound bursting through me, a desperate cry that makes me sound weak. It does nothing to stop them. Even Jasik does not look my way.

Now on all fours, he attempts to crawl away, but he is surrounded. The rogues mock his pain, his loss, but he pays them no attention. He moves slowly, digging his hands into the earth and worming his way closer to me. But I know he will never make it. Still, he tries, groaning each time he pulls his limp body across the ground.

I grind my teeth, my anger bubbling over, far past the boiling point. It washes over me quickly, completely, and I see nothing but fury and fire. The pain I feel watching my sire die is overrun with something new. The amulet sizzles against my skin, and the warmth spreads to every fiber of my being. I sense the darkness in every part of me, but I'm not sure I am fully aware of it. Because I don't care enough to stop it, to release my hold and relinquish the entity within.

I push upward, rising quickly. I slam my fist into the rogue's chest, eyes focused on the herd of rogue vampires at Jasik's side. My hands, blazing red, scorch through the rogue's flesh like flame to cotton. He screams as he dies, showering me in ash that will mingle with the dirt, becoming unrecognizable.

When I am done, no one will know what happened here, how many were lost.

It rises within me, burning my innards as it grows hotter with each passing second. Unable to contain it any longer, I throw my arms out before me—straight, stiff lines pointed directly at the rogues—and the fire fueled by my anger erupts all around us. It encircles the rogues, consuming everything in its path. They scream, and some even try to run, but my fire moves quickly. Even they know they never had a chance.

They are engulfed in flames, igniting quickly and burning swiftly, showering the ground in what remains. It takes no time at all for us to win this battle, but even after they are dead, I can still hear their screams.

My laugh mimics their high-pitched whines, their pleas for mercy, until it turns deep and dark. It is the darkness that laughs, not me, and I realize that I feel most alive when it is happy.

Still seeing red, I do not release the fire. I continue to scorch the earth, allowing the flames to travel farther from me and deeper into the forest. Beds of early rising flowers wilt, brush is resorted to ash, and flames lick the length of nearby trees. Seeing the destruction caused by my hands fills me with joy. The rogues deemed me weak, choosing to surround Jasik and not me, but I proved them wrong.

Jasik screams my name, voice scratchy and exasperated. I realize he is begging me to stop, but I ignore him, only obeying after he crawls to my side and grabs my leg, squeezing so hard I am forced to focus on him and not my magic.

Seeing my sire broken and bruised, I finally crumble, falling to my knees. Chest heaving, I struggle to calm my heavy heart. My vision is still blurred, the bright, flashing remnants of fire still flickering behind my eyes. The floating streaks and speckles of bright light are all I can see, but it slowly begins to clear.

Jasik pulls himself upright and grabs my hand. He leans against me, and I lend him my strength.

"Focus on me, on my touch," he says. "You can do this."

Confused, I frown, still breathing heavily. I follow his gaze and stare at my hands, where fire magic flew freely only moments ago. My palms are pale, skin soft from the heat of the flames, but my breath hitches when I see what Jasik sees.

Seeping from my arms is wispy darkness. The black, lacy swirls are slowly dying down as they return to the amulet. Black veins are etched into my skin where the smoke retreats. I watch as they move up my arms and onto my chest until finally retreating to the black onyx crystal.

Rather than using my own magic, I harnessed the magic stored there without meaning to, without even thinking about it. I meant to summon the elements, but somehow, the need to connect with the evil within overcame my sanity, and I allowed that evil to escape, to use my body as its own. Now, as I sever our connection, it is returning to the stone.

I am stunned, ashamed of my actions. I swipe at my forehead, now glittered with sweat. The longer I remain without that magic, the worse I feel. My muscles ache, my chest burns, and the pit in my stomach is slowly becoming a tight knot. My throat is coarse, my mind racing with panicked thoughts. I feel shaky and jittery, like I haven't fed in weeks. With the magic drained, I feel like death.

Jasik reaches forward, grazing his fingertips across the veins on my chest. They slowly dissipate, but he lingers, the silence between us so loud it hurts.

"This magic is changing you, Ava," he whispers.

"I didn't mean to use it," I say, voice cracking. "You have to believe me."

"You didn't mean to, yet you sought the darkness," he says, meeting my gaze. "That's what it wants. It wants you to harness the black magic, to become one with it."

"I'm scared," I admit.

"Promise me you'll never harness that magic again," he says.

I nod, but even though I feel his fear and concern, one raging thought loops in my mind.

When can I harness it again?

The manor emerges before us, ominous and threatening, like it already knows all my secrets. It probably does. Something about the way this house hovers makes it feel alive. The sharp, stark angles and dark exterior look eerie in the moonlight, the windows like eyes piercing straight through to my soul. If it knows my secrets, chances are, the others do too.

"We will need to tell them what happened with the girl and with . . . your magic," Jasik says. He hesitates when he speaks, like he is unsure of what actually happened, even though he witnessed the amulet's wrath.

I sigh heavily but nod in agreement. I would love to keep my slipup between just the two of us, but I don't ask him to agree to this. Because I already know his answer. He is a staunch supporter of honesty above all else, and in most circumstances, I agree with that mentality. But not tonight. I guess I'm just not ready to face my friends.

"Perhaps Holland or Sofía have come up with a way to safely destroy the amulet," he says, hopeful. It's what he doesn't say that gives me pause: *Maybe if they have found a way to destroy the amulet, Malik won't force you out.*

I don't respond, my mind too busy swirling around the conversation we didn't actually have. Still, the unspoken words rock me to my core.

"After what happened, you must see that you can't do this alone," he says sternly, misinterpreting my silence. "I know you want to. You are fiercely independent, much to your own demise."

"Amicia used to say I should admire the qualities you all seem to deem reckless," I say, instantly regretting my words.

Jasik is silent, lost to thoughts likely revolving around his dead sire. I know how much Amicia meant to him, and reminding him of her while we are still surrounded by so much uncertainty is a low blow.

"I'm sorry," I say. "I don't know what's wrong with me. I didn't mean to . . . I shouldn't have—"

"It's okay. I know you didn't mean it," he says.

"I'm just scared, and I'm taking it out on you. That's not right."

"You don't need to fear the amulet, Ava," he says. "We have every intention of keeping you safe."

"I'm not afraid of the amulet," I say too quickly. "I'm afraid of Malik."

My confession makes him stop, and he turns to face me fully. His features are hard, unreadable, so I continue. The last thing I want is to upset him further.

"I am worried this will push him over the edge," I say. "I

have tested his limits for too long, and now he will have no choice but to make me leave."

"After everything that has happened, that is what you are worried about?" he asks softly. I hear the humor in his voice. I suppose after nearly dying, then almost killing a human, and then practically merging with an evil entity we still know nothing about, my leader's disapproval should be the last thing I fear. Yet, even though I know this, I am still worried about my punishment.

"I admit it sounds silly, but I don't want to lose my family . . . *again*."

"Ava, if you are truly interested in destroying the amulet, Malik would not make you leave. I promise."

"How can you be so sure?" I ask. "He has been angry with me for so long. It is only a matter of time before—"

Jasik embraces me, silencing my anxiety, and I lean against him, finding comfort in his cool caress. There is something special about his touch; it makes me feel safe in a world intent on ending my life.

"Because I know my brother," he says, breath fluffing my hair. "All he wants is to protect his family, and you *are* family."

SEVEN

I am standing on the front walkway, watching as Jasik enters the manor without me. He closes the door behind him. I stare at it for several seconds before I continue forward. My legs are heavy, and I ascend slowly. Every bit of my anxiety has returned, despite just being comforted by Jasik.

When I reach the top landing, I turn back toward the forest. Perched on the porch, with my bottom resting on the top step, I let my legs dangle down before me. My boots are scuffed and dirty, my jeans ripped and caked with mud. My shirt is singed, my jacket tarnished by hours of tumbling through the brush. Even my hands bear the truth of battle. My skin is creamy and soft, but rather than pale in color, I am dusted in gray ash. I brush my palms together, never succeeding to completely remove the matter.

I sigh sharply and rest my elbows on my knees, staring out at the trees. Within them, our enemies hide, finding coverage and comfort in a place meant for the living. We may have killed most of the rogues who attacked tonight—losing only a few in retreat—but there are even more out there. They keep settling in this area, determined to make Darkhaven their home for good. Two separate rogue attacks in one night is no coincidence. These were coordinated events, and I'm well aware that Jasik and I are lucky to be alive.

I pick at my fingers, freeing some of the dirt beneath my nails, as I think about the rogues I fought tonight. They seemed intent on killing Jasik. In both attacks, more of the rogue vampires focused on him rather than on me. Why? I am used to being the one they fear, the one with the power they want, but they had little interest in fighting me. If anything, it was like they just wanted to keep me busy, force me out of the way so they can get to what they really want.

If that rogue didn't slip, if I didn't figure out what they were up to, Jasik would be dead right now. I let that thought sink in, resonating deep in my gut. A shiver worms its way through my spine despite the warm night air. The moonlight is shining down again, the clouds finally dispersing enough for me to see the stars. At the manor, I should be safe from rogue attacks, but I still feel uneasy, like the battle still isn't over.

The door behind me opens, a brush of stale air wafting toward me. I turn just in time to see Jasik return with a blood bag. He tosses it to me, and I catch it midair. My stomach grumbles at the sight, and I lick my lips involuntarily.

"I thought you might be hungry," he says. "It is important to feed after the night we had."

I nod, tearing my gaze from the blood bag to glance at my sire. In the moonlight, I see him more clearly. He took the brunt of both attacks tonight. His clothes are tattered and dirty, his skin pale and gray. I gasp when I notice the scorch marks. I had no idea my magic was dangerously close to consuming my sire too.

"Jasik," I whisper, unable to look away from just how exhausted he truly is.

"It's okay," he says. "*We* are okay, and we are home now. That is what matters."

I nod, but my emotions are still getting the best of me. I turn away, finding more comfort looking at the darkness beyond the manor than at my sire.

I toss his offering between my hands. The blood, swirling within, is mesmerizing. I rip open the blood bag with my teeth and drain it quickly. The liquid, thick and smooth, washes over me, consuming my senses. All at once, from its scent to its taste, blood overrides everything else.

The porch creaks as Jasik crouches beside me. He takes the empty bag from my hands and kisses my temple softly. I still don't look at him as he retreats, returning inside and closing the door behind him. My shame keeps me silent, and I worry I won't have the courage to stand up to whatever judgment Malik passes down.

I shimmy next to the gargoyle and look at my old friend. Dark gray and stained by years of elemental abuse, he simply stares into the distance, never giving me his attention. Maybe he is mad at me too.

"I need your strength tonight," I whisper.

I feel guilty for asking this of him because I abandoned him too. I was consumed by my hatred of the witch and my desire to protect the amulet at all costs. I was careless, forgetting about my friends—dead and alive. I don't deserve their forgiveness, even though I still yearn for it.

With my hand hovering over the gargoyle's head, ready to pat my way back into his stone heart, something catches my eye. I freeze, arm hovering in the air, as I focus on the shifting darkness in the distance.

I stand, descending the steps slowly, encroaching closer to what I fear is yet another rogue. A third coordinated attack sounds exhausting, even though I recently fed. The blood in my stomach is still working its way through my system, and until it has completely rejuvenated me, I will continue to feel the lingering effects of exhaustion.

The longer I stare, the harder it is to make out what I am looking at. My vision blurs, shadows morphing as the clouds roll by overhead. I continue walking through the yard, squinting so my eyes can better adjust to the ever-changing lighting.

When I reach the wrought-iron fence that surrounds our property, I hesitate to pass the threshold. How far is too far? How far can I safely travel before I am closer to foe than friend?

I take a hesitant step forward, bones nearly jumping out of my skin when I hear the front door behind me. It swings open, slamming against the house's siding, a crashing sound I am all too familiar with.

I spin on my heels, readying myself for an attack, only to find Malik standing in the doorway. He charges toward me. The others stay behind, but they appear just as angry. Their distance alone speaks volumes.

Hikari and Jeremiah wait on the bottom step, arms crossed, gazes cast downward. They stand in front of Holland and Sofía as though they are protecting *them* from *me*. Never have I felt so misunderstood, so out of place in the home that was meant to be mine for all eternity.

My gaze settles on Malik, and I brace myself, desperately trying to hide my panic over what is to happen. Because I believe this is it. This is the moment I have been preparing for—the fight, the ousting, the final brutal words spoken that cannot be taken back.

The emergence of Malik walking swiftly closer has woken

the amulet. I feel it stir against my skin, the warmth growing hotter with each step Malik takes toward me. I fear what it will do when cornered—what it will make *me* do.

I stumble backward, nearly tripping over my feet. The amulet is buzzing now, the sound growing so loud I can't even hear my stammering heart. A second ago, it was all I heard, canceling out the sound of the forest coming alive at night and even the distant, crashing waves of the sea. Now it has fallen mute, giving way to a louder sound: Malik's silence.

Malik speaks to me, but I hear nothing. He repeats himself. I watch his lips move, but I do not hear the sound that escapes them. Instead, I hear the blood rushing to my brain and the high-pitch siren call of the amulet. It is piercing and screechy, and it makes me shudder in agony. It feels like a thousand tiny pins pricking my inner ear, and the closer I am to the vampires, the deeper they burrow.

Still treading backward, I glance at the others, but they show no interest in stopping their leader. They remain on the porch, watching as Jasik and Malik rush toward me.

I stop walking backward when I bump into a tree, the sharp edges of pointed limbs stabbing into my spine. I wince and freeze, with Malik swiftly approaching. Trapped, I have nowhere to go. Either I turn and run, or I stay and fight. I make my decision just in time, choosing to trust my sire over the voice of doubt within.

"What have you done?" Malik hisses.

"Malik, stop," Jasik shouts. "Let her explain."

I notice the others remain silent, not coming to my defense the way Jasik has. Instead, they stand with Sofia. I don't bother looking at her, but I can imagine her happy glare, her mischievous smile. I'm sure my downfall brings her immense joy.

"Answer me!" Malik shouts, regaining my attention.

I shake my head, searching for the words to accurately describe the mess I have gotten myself into, but I come up short. Anything I say will be something he understands from personal experience—after all, he has experienced blood lust too—but won't excuse my actions. When it comes down to it, I put us all at risk—again.

"I—I'm . . . I'm sorry," I say, words and thoughts a jumbled mess.

I stare into his hard, crimson eyes, pleading with him to trust my apology, but he is emotionless. His eyes are narrowed, his anger fuming, and I can practically taste his distaste for me. I could explain that it was an accident, but he already knows that. He knows I wouldn't intentionally harm a human—or Jasik. But I fear that won't be enough.

"You are out of control," Malik shouts, arms flailing. "First, that damn amulet, then you risk us all by returning to your mother's house, and now you nearly kill a human."

"I didn't mean to hurt her!" I yell. "You have to believe me." My voice is scratchy and whiny.

"Give me the amulet," he says.

I knew it would come to this, but the surprise still washes over me. I instinctively grab the stone and cover it from prying eyes. I want to shield it with my hand, like that alone is all the protection it needs.

"Ava, I am not asking for permission," Malik says, voice icy. He glances from my eyes to where I'm holding the stone and back again. "Give it to me." He emphasizes each word slowly, carefully, and a chill spreads through my body at the sound of his voice.

When I try to speak, I am silenced. My throat feels like

it is closing. I struggle to breathe through the invisible grasp muting me by swallowing gulps of air when I am able to, but it is not enough. I choke on my words, heart hammering in my chest, and my vision blurs as I fight back tears. I feel light-headed and woozy, and I begin to shake. I think I might truly pass out.

"Now," Malik orders. "You must give it to me now!"

"Please give it to him, Ava," Jasik says.

His voice is calm but insistent. It feels like it grounds me in place, yet I am unsteady on my feet. I teeter from side to side, slowly sinking into the earth where I stand. The soil is soft and mushy, and it clings to my heels, coating my boots in its grasp. The longer I stand like this, the harder it is to fight. It feels like I am hovering over my body, watching our encounter, utterly incapable to intervene.

"We have no intention of harming you," Jasik reminds me.

He is louder now, like he may be walking closer, but my vision is so cloudy I can't see them anymore. The world before me is cloaked in darkness, blurred and unrecognizable.

I see their shadowy figures moving closer, but I am unable to reach for them. I am numb, paralyzed within my own skin, but the phantom pain lingers, reminding me that while I may *feel* lonely, I am not alone. The darkness is *always* there.

Only when I feel its grasp loosening am I able to respond.

"I can't," I whisper between haggard breaths. My throat is coarse and scratchy. It hurts to speak, to swallow, even to breathe.

"Yes, you can," Malik says calmly. "Just release it. That's all you need to do. Let it go, and I will take it."

I try to obey, but my arms are shaking. My muscles strain from how hard I am clutching the crystal. I fear it may fracture beneath my grasp. I am breathing heavy and loud, the air penetrating my lungs like knives to my chest.

Everything aches. Slowly, sliver by sliver, I feel my body being stripped away, sliced open, raw and fleshy.

"You don't understand," I say, voice screechy. "He won't let me."

My confession shatters through the echoing sound of everything around us, silencing my erratic heart, my hissing breath, my pounding head. The world falls mute—even my friends halt—as I process my words.

He won't let me, I think again, and from within the black onyx crystal, he wakes.

Time stops, the world moving forward at an agonizingly slow pace. The hunters begin their ascent toward me, forming a line behind Malik. Their maneuver reminds me of the rogue attack—that crescent-shaped line. I glance at Sofía. She alone remains on the steps, and when our gazes meet, she smiles at me. All at once, my hatred for her is renewed, but now, something inside of me relishes in the innate spite I have for her.

Malik is only an arm's reach away now. Jasik is at his side, but his attention is on his brother, not me. I don't bother with either of them. I keep my eyes focused on Sofía, on the slow beat of the vein in her neck and on the sound of blood coursing through it. I lick my lips.

Malik lunges forward, arm dashing outward. My jacket is open, my shirt cut low enough for me to feel the moment my leader's fingers brush against my skin. I am still clinging to the amulet, so he clasps his hand around mine. He tries to tug my arm away, attempting to pull the amulet with it.

Everything happens so quickly, only seconds passing by,

but that is all it takes. Malik attacks, and the amulet reacts.

I release my grasp, but the chain never breaks. I swing my arm around, forcing Malik's to the side, and with my other hand, I send him flying through the air. I make impact with his chest, listening for the distinct cracking noise that convinces me I damaged bone. He will survive the assault, but he will also need time to heal.

He still soars through the air, landing on the others. They fall to the ground in a messy pile of limbs bent at awkward angles. Holland cries out, distracting Jeremiah. Hikari is focused on Malik, leaving Jasik the only vampire at my side.

"You're not well, Ava," my sire cautions, but I ignore him. Not well? I have never felt better. But of course, Jasik could never understand how freeing this feels. The hunters happily live their lives in cages, restraining their natural desires.

Likely realizing I have no intention of continuing a verbal duel, he tries to forcefully take the amulet. He makes the same mistake his brother made, but somehow, I am surprised by his actions. I expected better from the vampire who made me what I am.

Jasik reaches for the stone, but I shift slightly. He misses the amulet, fisting air, and I grab on to him. I clasp his hand within my own, squeezing tightly. His hand is much larger than mine, but the tiny bones encased in his skin will still give way to greater strength. And I am far stronger than he can even imagine.

Smiling, I close the space between us, and with each step, I grasp his hand tighter. He winces as I do this, grinding his teeth. With his jaw clenched, the tiny muscles in his face twitch, but he never vocalizes his pain. I suppose that is what an eternity has taught him: how to hide—his emotions, his strength, his desires. He hides everything he is, everything he wants to be. In this moment, when I am truly free, his envy for me must be eating him up inside.

He tries to free himself by pulling away, but I never release my grasp. Instead, I grab him by the neck with my free hand, lowering him to his knees. I am not gentle with him, so his kneecaps smack the earth in a loud thud. He uses his free hand to scratch at my arm, desperate for me to release his throat.

"It would be so easy for me to end your life," I say.

My voice is dark, deep, laced in malice and hunger. I yearn for him in ways I never have before. I ache for his blood, for it to cascade over my body as he slowly bleeds out. I have no desire to taste him. I just want to watch him take his last breath.

"Ava," he says, but he doesn't sound the same either. He chokes on my name, voice raspy and weak. He tries to say something else, maybe a promise that he doesn't want to hurt me. I see that confession in his eyes, even though the words do not leave his lips, and the thought makes me happy. I decide I will answer him.

I lean close, sharing what little breath I allow him to inhale. Our noses touch, lips graze. His eyes close.

"You haven't the power to stop me," I say.

He opens his eyes as I begin to pull away, and he chokes out another breath.

"Look at your . . . " he begins, hacking. He does not finish, and I don't care to understand what he means.

The earth begins to rumble. At first, I believe I am doing this, that my power is so strong even I cannot contain it. I am quickly disappointed when I realize it is not shifting because of my elemental control. The vampires are doing this. They are rushing toward me, likely intent on saving their fallen comrade.

I drop Jasik's wounded hand and place my palm against his head. I look at him as I do this, and something passes between us—a truth, a confession of what is to come. He understands my intention, and still, I see the pity in his eyes.

I twist suddenly, sharply, and with the quick expel of air and rushed gasp of his shock—like he knew what was coming but still didn't expect me to do it—my sire falls limp in my arms. I grab him at the back of the neck and toss his motionless body aside, fully facing the others.

I step forward as they scream Jasik's name. Their voices are pained, as they too share his surprise. It seems everyone in that house underestimated me.

As I pass by the wrought-iron gate, I grab one of the metal rods. The top is adorned with two sharp slabs in the form of a cross, and when it comes into contact with my skin, I am burned. I seethe, sucking air through my clenched teeth. It makes a loud hissing sound, but I do not release the cross.

I feel the symbol being burned into my skin, etched as a scorching reminder that I am not merely a hybrid anymore. I am becoming something far more powerful. As I merge with the darkness encased in stone, I notice several things, the most important of which is that the entity within the amulet has completely absorbed the power of my coven, becoming stronger and more fierce than anything I have ever faced. Pairing its strength with my own will make me unstoppable. Never before have I desired such dominance, elite leadership over the land.

I pull the metal rod free from the ground and swing it forward, releasing it so it soars toward my assailants. It slices through the air, a steady swooshing sound that ceases only when the tip of the cross penetrates Jeremiah's torso. His flesh caves with a deep, wet sucking sound as the cross lodges within his chest.

The moment the rod makes impact, Jeremiah is flung backward. He slams into the side of the manor and crumbles to the ground, his anguish music to my ears. Humming, I raise my arms and sway from side to side like I am orchestrating the music he creates.

Holland rushes to Jeremiah's side, pulling out the dagger from Jeremiah's chest with a loud huff. The vampire's flesh is seared from the contact, the cross burning through to bone. I imagine it will take quite some time for him to heal, which means he is effectively out of my way and left to watch his friends perish.

Jeremiah breathes erratically, heavily, and for a moment, it is all I can hear. It is so annoyingly distracting that I consider ending his pain quickly, but I am reminded that there is no fun in mercy.

Holland is crouched beside Jeremiah and begins whispering to his fallen lover—maybe words of encouragement, maybe a healing spell. I don't care enough to make out what he says. Either way, the witch won't be speaking long either.

Hikari and Malik are closing in on me. They rush forward in unison. I suppose Malik has forgotten that I spent months training with him. There is nothing he can do to stop me, no battle plan I have not been taught.

Hikari lunges first. Like an acrobat, she springs upward and soars back down, foot angled to be planted squarely against my chest. I have seen this maneuver a hundred times before. She grunts as she locks her knee, leg pointed outward, but as we make contact, I barely budge. I chuckle at her failed attempt to subdue me. She falls to the ground, landing awkwardly on her back, and gasps. On her bottom, she tries to crawl away from me as I hover over her.

Malik reaches my side, but since I am not yet done with Hikari, I slam the back of my balled fist against his jaw. His neck snaps back. A wet, sticky grunt escapes his chest as he falls to the ground, motionless. He lies only a few feet from his brother, but I pay them both no attention.

My body is sizzling, humming and buzzing with excitement, but I don't dare take my eyes off Hikari. I shake away the sensation and refocus on the cowering vampire, as heat from the amulet spreads across my chest. The constant buzzing in my ears almost completely drowns out her pleas, much to my gratitude.

"Ava, listen to me," she says breathlessly. "It chose you because you're strong. That means you can fight it."

I cock my head to the side and smile.

"But I don't want to fight it," I say softly.

"It needs you, Ava," she says quickly. "That means you have power over it."

"No, but you know who I do have power over?" I ask, voice deepening. "You."

I summon the elements, a fireball sparking to life within the palm of my hand. I bounce it playfully, enjoying Hikari's shock. She isn't looking at me anymore. Her gaze remains focused on the flame within my hand, eyes wide with fear. They move every time I fling it in the air.

"Please don't do this," she says, still not looking at me.

But she's too late. The moment she asks for me to spare her life, I am already committed to ending her.

Something hits my chest, and I stumble backward, losing control over my own magic. My fireball flings to the side, narrowly missing Hikari's face.

She scurries backward and jumps to her feet, and another force hits me in the chest. This happens again and again, pushing me farther and farther away from my intended target.

The more it happens, the more I feel the heat of it. I hear the sizzle of my jacket burning, the smell of my flesh cooking. My clothes are singed, my flesh bright red and stark black— somehow at the same time.

I glance up in time to see the next force slam against me. It is a fireball, and this time, I lose my footing, stumbling backward and tripping over Jasik's unmoving body. I fall to the ground, and when I open my eyes, I stare into my sire's seemingly lifeless irises.

I feel nothing.

I push him away and claw to my feet, snarling loudly, saliva dripping down my chin as I growl in anger. Another fireball soars through the air, but now that I am expecting the attack, I dodge it easily. I scan the area for my assailant, my vision landing on Sofía, who is now standing at the bottom of the stairs.

"I hoped it would be you," I say through gritted teeth.

Holland is on the ground beside her, and he cradles Jeremiah to his chest.

Hikari is slowly making her way toward Malik, who remains unconscious beside his brother.

I give her no attention, allowing her to pull her friends to what she believes is safety. For now, my focus is solely on Sofía, the witch I have wanted to kill since the moment she arrived in Darkhaven.

Sofía summons another fireball and holds it for me to see. She bounces it in her palm, tauntingly, much like I did with

Hikari only moments ago. I suppose she thinks she is scaring me.

"It will take more than another fireball to stop me," I warn.

"I'm just getting started," she hisses.

"Good," I say with a smile. "So am I."

I throw my arms out to my sides and summon the energy stored in the amulet. It erupts from within the stone, pouring outward and torching the earth it passes. The power bursts outward, and I nearly lose my footing as I struggle to maintain the steady stream of heat and energy.

The source of magic coming from the stone is the color of obsidian, but in the moonlight, it morphs into dark, shimmery swirls of unhindered madness. There are lacy puffs of smoke and steam swarming through it, tainting the area around the stream in darkness. It buzzes loudly, penetrating my mind with thoughts of death and blood and chaos.

Almost more than I can bear, I arch my back as the energy surges forward, using my body as its vessel, but the moment the surge of darkness reaches the manor, where my friends await destruction, it is stopped. I squint, struggling to see through the wave of black magic that pours from the stone. But when I see it, I gasp.

A bright-white iridescent shield of light envelops the front of the house. It first emerged as a small, thin layer of protection directly between the darkness and the manor, but it has grown. The longer the amulet releases the entity's power, the larger and thicker the shield becomes.

It cascades light around the front of the house, protecting the hunters who lie just behind its surface. The force of the shield stopping the energy from within the amulet sends me skidding backward, the impact jolting and vibrating through my limbs.

I dig my heels into the dirt, succeeding only in uprooting more soil. I slam against the very tree that trapped me early, but this time, I welcome its embrace. But even this tree cannot keep me safe. The longer I stand against it, pinned in place, the weaker the tree becomes.

The distant, resonating sound of the trunk giving way erupts around me. It splits, a long, deep gash in the bark bursting from within. The tree sways and cracks, leaning backward and upending roots, nearly toppling over completely.

With each passing second, I grow more exhausted. The amulet begins to falter, the darkness giving way to light. The weaker I become, the better I feel. My mind begins to clear, and the hold the entity has over me wanes.

The swirling, wispy black magic is sucked back into the stone as I release the amulet's power and slide to the ground. I land firmly at the base of the tree. Body shaking, chest heaving, mind numb as the events of these past several minutes replay in my head.

I look at my friends, each broken in his or her own way. Holland clings to Jeremiah, who is slowly healing from having the cross lodged in his gut. Hikari is squatted in front of Malik and Jasik, who still slumber. Soon, they will wake, their bodies healed from my attacks, but the pain, the fear, the anger in their eyes may never dissipate. Like the others, they will stare at me with distrust.

I stand on wobbly legs and take an unsteady step forward, but my friends stop me.

"Don't," Hikari says, voice cold as ice.

"Just leave," Holland says, tears streaming down his face as he holds Jeremiah's head against his chest.

"I . . . I didn't mean—"

I stumble through an apology as I begin walking away, rushing backward until the space between us is so great I can no longer see the hatred in their glares.

EIGHT

I am running through the forest, the wind harsh at my heels. There is no one chasing me, but I am desperate to put distance between the manor and me. So I run.

I run until my legs burn and my feet are numb. I run until my heart feels like it will burst from my chest, my mind foggy from exertion. I run until I can't hear my friends anymore because the rhythmic beat of my feet smacking the earth is loud enough to drown out even the weakest whispers.

When I finally stop, I find myself in a familiar place. It wasn't difficult to locate the area where Jasik and I fought rogue vampires earlier tonight. I left my mark on this place, and it is forever tainted by my power.

The ground has been scorched, the fire from the amulet reaching as far as the top of nearby trees. Everything is charred and black and dead, left to decay among the rest of the brush.

The flowers have turned to ash, and the trees that managed to survive have wilted leaves, flimsy and unrecognizable from the extreme heat.

Evidence of rogues having died here is gone, like ashes in the wind, and I am alone. I suppose I should be used to the feeling, the sinking depression that clings to my heels, burrowing my frail frame even deeper in the mush. The loneliness clings to my chest, tightening its grip so hard I can barely breathe. Ever since I transitioned, I have felt little else. From being cast away by my coven to being ousted by my nestmates, I suppose I must be prepared to face the rest of my days in solitude. But an eternity alone sounds horrendous. I am not sure how anyone could live like that.

Jasik once told me he and his brother never really understood how well they have it, both birthed to this world by biological parents. As vampires, we eventually create our own families, but we are never born to each other by blood—only by lust. We experience that innate sensual desire to share the gifts we have, to promise each other an eternity of days and nights spent huddled together, shielded from the sun yet livened by the moon. He is aware that they have it better than others, but they don't truly understand the seclusion we feel, knowing our blood relatives are long gone or soon dying.

Thinking about my nestmates sends my heart into the pit of my gut. I have lived with witnessing their anger and pain over what I have done, and while I hate that I make them feel this way, I am slowly getting used to their disappointment. What I have never seen is their fear—in *me*. Of what I am. Of what I have done. Of what I *can* do. *They* fear *me*. Making them feel as though I would hurt them is unforgivable, so knowing I actually *have* hurt them is killing me.

I want their forgiveness, but I know it will not come easily. I need proof that something epic is happening here, in our small, idyllic village that no one has heard of. Something dangerous is afoot, and for some reason, the others are blinded to it. If I am the only one who can see, then it is up to me to free them from this haze.

I think about everything that happened since my coven was murdered, but thinking about them only leads me to the rogue vampire I killed at the manor. With his striking crimson eyes, icy skin, and ruthless demeanor, just the thought of him sends chills down my spine. It feels like he is still haunting me, still hovering over the physical world, plaguing each decision I make with bad deeds.

The amulet reacts to the thought of him by warming against my skin. It wants me to remember the moment I killed him, the time I harnessed its power to take his life. It wants me to remember, and it wants me to enjoy it. What truly scares me is that I *do* like killing rogues, but does that make me a monster? Am I damned for wanting to rid the world of evil?

I try not to think about the way my heart yearns for another kill. Instead, I focus on the rogue I killed and the mysterious dreamwalker who still wears a mask. I haven't had a vision in several nights. The man warning me of the dangers of the amulet stopped appearing in my dreams as soon as I started to merge with it, harnessing its power as my own. Maybe he knows what I have done. Maybe he knows, and maybe he too has given up on me.

I try to remember what the rogue said just before I killed him. He said something about making a promise to keep me safe. He said he wasn't supposed to kill me, but I threatened his ego. I embarrassed him in front of the others, and he would make me pay for that.

I spent most of that battle fighting only him, which didn't occur to me until tonight. The rogues Jasik and I encountered today seemed to have similar orders. They were more focused on keeping me busy while the majority went after my sire.

I tell myself there is no such thing as coincidences in Darkhaven. In a place like this, one that is bursting with magic and so secluded from the rest of the world, everything is connected. Things happen with purpose here. They are intentional and masterminded. That means the attacks today must be linked to the original rogue vampire I fought and killed before.

I think about Sofía, about her purpose in all of this. My blood boils at the thought of her, and I struggle to maintain my composure. I think her name, and instantly I want to summon the strongest winds, the fiercest fire, the deepest water. I want to upheave this world with magic and watch it crumble beneath its weight.

Body shaking, muscles tense, I try to control my fury. I am coming to the realization that my hatred for her is amplified by the amulet. It boosts my anxiety and my anger, using it against me during my weakest moments. It is turning me into something I'm not, into someone I don't want to be. The others have seen these moments when I submit to the darkness and allow it to seethe from my lips, and I am ashamed. Still, I worry about her, about her true intentions for Darkhaven. Being wrong risks everything I have ever known. But after today, I am starting to see why the others trust her. She stopped me from doing any real harm to my friends. She saved their lives, and I am not sure I can ever repay that debt. It is forgiveness I seek, but surely she won't grant me such pleasure.

I have been certain of her allegiance to the dark side, but if Sofía truly isn't in league with the rogues, then she was telling the truth. She came here to hunt, to search for the rogue vampire who stole her family and upended her life. I can relate to that. Seeking my revenge is what fueled me for so long. She may not be as evil as I portrayed her. If I wasn't so immediately defensive of her, I might have called her a friend.

But that doesn't mean these rogue attacks aren't connected. They must be. None of them, from *three* separate attacks, seemed interested in killing me, which means they were getting protection orders from someone else. Even though I witnessed it with my own eyes, it still seems impossible.

I was once told rogues lack control and leadership—this is what makes them so different from us. Their blood lust gets in the way, becoming the sole thing they care about. They may live in nests like we do, but rarely do they have a single leader making all their decisions, like we had with Amicia and now with Malik. That means the vampire leading them must be truly powerful. It would take someone strong and smart to maintain order, to pass down judgment and watch it play out. But who? Amicia was the oldest vampire I have ever met, and even she didn't believe rogues were capable of leadership.

What's worse is that the dreamwalker has to be connected somehow to the rogue attacks. If he is a witch, trapped and held against his will, using his magic to reach me, I need to help him, to save him from certain death. If he is a witch who sold his soul to rogues, then I must stop him. Either way, I need to find him, and the only way I will find answers is by finding the rogue nest.

During our battles, a few rogues fled. Maybe I can track them somehow. Maybe they will unwittingly lead me right to their nest. And if the dreamwalker is involved, he will be there. He may even be waiting for me, knowing I would one day find their hideout. Darkhaven is only so big; it shouldn't take weeks to locate their lair.

The longer I work through my mental process of figuring out how to get myself out of this mess, the hotter the amulet becomes. Finally, when the heat is unbearable, I suck in a sharp breath, skin sizzling.

As I rub my wounded skin, crystal resting against my fingers, I begin to think about Sofía, the uncertainty of her intentions making me nervous. And a single thought begins looping in my mind.

What if Sofía is involved? If she is connected, finding the dreamwalker may be the proof I need to convince the others. She may even be responsible for my lack of control. For so long, I have blamed the amulet for influencing me, but maybe it's the witch.

I scratch at my skin, listening as the soft, deep voice whispers in my mind. The amulet bounces against the back of my hand, burning my skin. It heals quickly, but the buzzing, like a thousand hornets swarming my head, never goes away.

Jasik finds me sitting at the center of the charred remains from our earlier battle. I am cross-legged and swaying from side to side, thoughts of scorned witches and evil intentions repeating in my mind. It is all I can think about, and every time I try to pull away, to free myself from the endless loop, I am stopped by that deep, dark voice within.

He kneels before me, and I see him, but I do not believe he is there. I think my mind is playing tricks on me again, showing me what I want while whispering what I need.

"Ava?" he says, voice warm and smooth and deep. It penetrates my heart, and I whimper at the familiar sound.

I am almost too scared to speak—fearing if I do, I will break our connection and he will disappear forever. So I close my eyes, allowing my vampire senses to stretch outward, passing my body, rushing like a wave over the surrounding area.

I inhale deeply, letting the scent of the land and its people fill my lungs. I listen to the long, slow sounds of nature. I can even hear the humans of Darkhaven, but I sense nothing else in the woods. No rogues. No hunters. Nothing besides Jasik and me and the short distance between us.

"Are you okay?" he asks, speaking slowly. Even with my eyes closed, I can see him in my mind. He is treading closer, voice growing louder. His footsteps make the ground shake, the vibrations resonating deep within my crossed legs.

I whisper his name. I want to say many things to him. I want to apologize for what I did, for the mess I have caused. I want to explain what happened, because all he has heard are the stories the others told him. He has to know I never meant to hurt them.

"Open your eyes," he says, voice rich and smooth.

I obey, meeting his gaze. He is crouched in front of me, clothes bloodstained and singed from our previous fight. His skin is pale and soft, his neck smooth and untouched. The bones encased there have healed, the physical reminder of our encounter long gone.

I want to say so many things to him, but I don't. Suddenly, the fear that we are being watched is all I can think about. It gnaws at my innards, making my skin prickle and hair stand on end. I glance back at him, scanning the distance, but I see nothing. Still, that does not mean they aren't out there, watching, waiting.

"Are you alone?" I ask.

He nods. "Are you?"

His words make me think about the amulet, so I glance down to where it rests. I am still holding it, still scratching at my skin. Blood drips down my chest, and my shirt is soaked. My hand is splattered in crimson liquid, skin stained. My nails have dug burrows in my flesh, and my body is struggling to heal the torn flesh. Jasik places a hand over mine, encouraging me to stop. I obey, but I do not lower my hand.

"You're hurting yourself," he says softly. "You have to stop now. Okay?"

I nod, swallowing the knot in my throat. I want him to move his hand, to put distance between us. Until he does, I won't lower my arm. My palm hovers over the stone, never touching but always shielding. I must keep it safe.

"You're too close," I whisper.

Still crouching in front of me, he leans back, but the space is enough for my nerves to settle. I lower my arm, only then realizing how much my muscles ache.

"How did you find me?" I ask.

"I'll always find you," he says.

"I'm sorry," I say. "For what I did."

"I know," he says.

He smiles at me, and I believe him. I know he has forgiven me. He holds out his hand, and I stare at it. Fingers long and slender, his arm doesn't shake. His offering is sincere.

"Let's go home."

"I can't go back. They don't want me there."

"They will understand," he counters.

I notice how soft his voice sounds, how monotone and robotic. I don't like it, and it makes me frown.

"We just want to help you," he says.

"They tried to help me. Look what happened."

"That was my fault," he says. "I should have known it couldn't handle direct confrontation. I should have stopped

Malik before it got that far."

"I am going to fix this," I say. "I am going to make it right again."

"Ava, you can't do this alone," he reminds me. "Please, let me help you."

I shake my head. Feeling trapped, I stand and step backward. He rises with me, still giving me space but never really moving away. It makes me feel uneasy. I can tell the amulet doesn't like it either because it is warm against my skin.

"No, you saw what happened before," I argue. "I can't risk that happening again. Next time . . . "

I trail off, the silence stretching on for far too long.

"Next time, you might kill me," he says, finishing my sentence.

His words pierce my heart. My vision blurs from the threat of tears, so I just nod. I would never intentionally harm Jasik, but I wouldn't hurt the others either. Still, it happened.

"I wouldn't be here if I thought you were capable of that," he says.

"Not me. *It*," I say, mirroring his words from earlier. "I worry what *it* will do if confronted by you."

"If it wanted me dead, it would have killed me before."

"We don't know that," I say. "Maybe you're right, but if you're wrong, it will cost you your life. Are you prepared to make that bargain?"

"For you, I would pay that cost a hundred times over if I could," he says.

"I don't deserve such loyalty," I whisper. I reach for him, hand falling short of making the connection. He notices this and steps forward, closing the space between us.

"Let me help you."

"You can't," I say.

"How will you do this alone?"

"I can fix this. I already have a plan. I just need time to find the dreamwalker," I say, the words spilling from me faster than I can keep up with them. They come out jumbled and messy, chaotic but true.

If the dreamwalker is an innocent bystander in all of this, then he has the power to destroy the amulet. After all, he was strong enough to enter my dreams uninvited, which is no easy feat. And if he is responsible, then killing him will resolve a lot of our issues. Holland and I will still need to find a way to dispose of the amulet, but at least our rogue problem will be taken care of. Finding the rogue nest is a win-win. It's just easier said than done.

Of course, I don't bother explaining all of this to Jasik. There isn't enough time. I am not even sure I have enough time to locate the rogue nest and return to the manor before sunrise. As much as I would love to spend the rest of the night in Jasik's arms, I can't. Too much is at risk now.

"What are you talking about?" he asks. "Who is the dreamwalker?"

"I don't have time to explain," I shout, exasperated. "But I need to find him before sunrise. He can help. *This will help!*"

"You're not making sense, Ava," Jasik says. "Who is the dreamwalker? When did you meet him? How can he help?"

"I'm sorry, but I have to go."

"Wait," he says as I begin to back away. "Please. Let me go with you. I am worried about you. You aren't well."

"You can't," I say. "Until I find the dreamwalker, no one is safe around me. I won't let anyone else be exposed to it."

I think about the text I read at Luna's store from the book

that's now hidden in my bedroom, the one that lists all the uses of black onyx in different cultures around the world. I grasp the stone now, running my thumb over its rough edges. This stone may be containing a powerful, evil vessel, but it also may be the cure for vampirism. I have to safely destroy the entity while also restoring the crystal's natural power. If Jasik understood what is at stake, he wouldn't stop me, but there isn't enough time to explain all of this—not if I want to find the nest before sunrise. All I know is I can't risk Jasik touching it. Not until I understand how it works.

"You have to trust me," I say, mind rapid-firing the list of things I need to do—and all before sunrise. "I am going to fix this. I want to kill the rogues, help the dreamwalker, get rid of Sofía, and finally destroy the amulet once and for all."

"Sofía?" he asks, confused. "Ava, you have to stop this. You have to stop fighting her. It is destroying you!"

"I have to leave," I say, walking backward and ignoring his cries.

Jasik dashes forward, eliminating the distance between us in quick, easy strides. He is in front of me now, grabbing my arm by the wrist. He clasps his hand over my bone, holding firmly. His gaze drops to the amulet, and I know what he plans to do. Like the others, he wants to take it, but he can't. It is mine.

"No!" I shout.

I jut the base of my palm outward and slam it against his chest so hard it forces the air from his lungs in a wet, sloppy gasp. His eyes widen in surprise, and he soars through the air, slamming to the ground several yards away. The earth craters where he lands, carving a deep gash into the soil and rooting him in place. It eased his fall, but I am not worried about that now.

The amulet buzzes loudly, humming against my chest. It is warm, the heat spreading like wildfire through my skin. The whisper-soft hissing from the entity within is all around me, and I know I am surrounded by its wispy black magic. I didn't intend to harness it, yet it was released. It seeped out on its own, using my fear and anger against me.

Jasik grunts as he stands, brushing off his clothes that are now covered in dirt. He glances at me, eyes unreadable. I know he is okay. I barely wounded him, but the reality of my attack is there. And he won't forget it.

"I have to go," I say sharply.

I leave him there, and I never look back.

I am in the midst of a field. Early wildflowers in shades of violet decorate the ground, which is otherwise covered in dead grass and decaying brush, remnants of a long, brutal winter season. The field is bordered by trees, all swaying to the beat of the wind's silent drum. The forest spills into this clearing, and I stand at its center, recognizing it immediately. Somehow, I always end up here.

The field looks different when I am not asleep, visiting this place via the astral plane. Spirit comes alive here, and I feel its presence even now. Unlike my friends, it is not disappointed with me. It is simply there, existing in the trees that move, the wind that blows. Spirit is the rocks in the earth, the soil that nourishes the plants. It is part of everything, everyone.

The wildflower field from my nightmares looks eerie in the moonlight, much like it does in most of my visions. I am alone, but the sway of the trees makes me feel like I am surrounded. The wind increases, blowing the clouds overhead so they cover the stars. The world darkens, and for a second too long, I am cloaked in the night.

It won't take long for Jasik to track me here. Unlike the rogues I seek, I left a rather obvious trail. The only thing keeping him away is my request, and I pray he abides by my wishes—if for nothing else, he must for his safety. The amulet can't be trusted. Not when it is so easily and unintentionally summoned.

I think about my options, knowing there are too few. I could try a locater spell, but I don't know who I am searching for. I don't know the identity of the dreamwalker, and I don't have anything of his to help guide the spell to him.

I am alone, with only the clothes on my back and the amulet at my chest, to help me through this. As much as I hate the idea, I know what I have to do. For what I hope will be the final time, I must harness the magic within the stone, using it to expand my senses and locate the rogue vampires.

I grasp the crystal. It feels weighty in my hand, even though it is so small. Almost the same size as my smallest finger, it doesn't appear to be as powerful as it is. An onlooker would never believe it contains such a dark being, let alone be the answer to curing vampirism.

I close my eyes, and I can see the madness within the stone. The depths of the crystal are vast, and within the stone casing, the evil entity has grown. It's consumed the power of my coven, and it is only a matter of time before it steals mine as well. My power, paired with its own, will be enough to free it. This, I am sure. I don't have to wonder what the entity will do with its freedom. I already know. I have experienced its desire for death, for power, firsthand.

I try not to think about what I am doing as I merge with the magic stored inside the amulet. I use it to fuel my own heightened senses, stretching out like wildfire over the land. I steer clear of the village—sensing too many humans in such a heightened state will be too much for me right now. The last thing I need is to relive my misstep with Luna.

I remain focused on the forest, assuming the rogue nest is hidden somewhere under the protection and coverage of the trees. I extend farther, growing more exhausted by the second. The longer I hold on to the power, harnessing it as my own, the weaker I become, but I refuse to give up. I didn't risk everything to get nothing in return.

Finally, when my resolve begins to falter, I sense something. A few lone figures are camped at the far edge of the forest in an area rarely hiked even by the humans of Darkhaven. I don't think I have ever patrolled as far as the woods would allow, which makes this particular spot the perfect base for our rogue population. The territory is vast and unexplored, making for safer vampire conditions.

With the information I need attained, I slowly begin releasing the power. It flutters through my chest and is sucked back into the amulet. I feel it work its way through my system, my guilt and disgust for allowing it to use my body overriding everything else. As it leaves me, it feels like worms burrowing through the soil, desperate to stay hidden even as fingers are pulling them free from the ground.

When it is back within the amulet, I clutch my chest, hand brushing the stone. When my skin makes contact with the crystal, it zaps me, a harsh, abrupt shock that radiates up my arm. I hiss in response, shaking my hand to ease the pain. This doesn't work, so I inspect my palm, noticing the deep gash etched into my skin.

"What the ... " I say, trailing off. Slowly, I am healing, my vampire abilities taking control, stopping the bleeding, and tethering new flesh with old. Even after the wound is gone, I still stare, unbelieving.

It almost felt like a warning, as though the entity within the amulet has no intention of being used solely for my purposes. We both want something out of this relationship, but what the darkness asks of me is more than I can offer.

NINE

I stand outside the entrance to the cave, suddenly overwhelmed by my flight instinct. After locating the rogue nest, I decided to investigate, but it took longer than expected to hike here.

There are ample manmade trails in the forest that surround the village, but none reach this far out. I was forced to trek through decades of brush to reach caves I didn't even know existed, and now, the sun is dangerously close to rising. The sky is growing lighter by the second, and I fear I won't have enough time to make it to shelter.

I have risked everything to find this nest, and even though I am itching to turn around, I know I can't. I won't be welcomed back until I prove myself to the others. I need something, *anything* to convince them to let me stay, to assure them that we have the same end goals. There is no better way to do this than by finding the dreamwalker and destroying the amulet.

I can't leave empty-handed, but knowing that still doesn't make investigating the caves any easier. I will have to camp here, sticking to the shadows until nightfall. Hopefully, they won't ever know I was here.

Years ago, when I was still a child, my mother told me the greatest magic comes in times of darkness, when a witch has no choice but to trust his or her own power. Today, I will rely heavily on the elements—something I haven't done in a long, long time. The realization makes me feel weak, like I am still a novice just now learning the importance of perfecting my craft.

I take my first hesitant step forward, inching closer to the entrance of the cave. Inside, I see only darkness. I hear nothing but the distant rumble of rogue vampires; they are rowdy and loud, uncaring that they may be heard. I am not sure how many there are, but I am fairly certain I will be severely outnumbered.

Access to the cave itself is short but wide. I will have to crouch and shimmy under the low overhang in order to enter. There are trees above the small opening, making the threshold look more like a hole an animal burrowed than the entrance to a labyrinth of tunnels.

Vegetation grows wild all around the opening, a vast covering of dull green moss blanketing the ground. Early rising wildflowers are in bloom, decorating the otherwise drab landscape in color.

The sensation that I am being watched makes my skin prickle. The uneasy feeling nestles deep in my gut, so I stand and spin, scanning the distance, but there is nothing but trees. I am far from town, from the manor, from any help at all. I am well aware that one of two things will happen once I enter this cave: I will succeed and live to see another day, or I will not. I try not to think about the latter as I crawl into the dark pit.

Tree roots dangle from the top of the cave, and I have to navigate through them without making a sound. Some are thick and unyielding, like they were here long before Darkhaven even became a place where people settled. Others are flimsy and thin, and I brush them away easily.

The deeper I explore, the smaller the channel becomes. No longer able to crawl, I slide on my stomach through the narrowest underpass. Even though there is no light, forcing me to rely on my heightened vampire senses, I can tell I am moving downward, using gravity to assist my descent.

The muttering squeaks of rats are all around me, and I can't tell if there is only one or if there are hundreds. Either way, I try not to think about it as I claw my way closer toward a single hint of light.

Once through the initial avenue of tree roots and dirt, I tumble ungracefully into the first section of the cave, falling several feet down to the rocky ground beneath. I grunt as I try to stop my fall with my arms, wincing at the sharp pain resonating in my wrists when flesh meets stone.

I peer up, praying I did not just fall into the laps of a dozen rogue vampires. The Gods must be on my side today, because I am alone—wounded, dirty, and exhausted, but alone. It's a real treat.

I stand, dusting off my hands. My palms are scratched, and my clothes are caked in muck. Otherwise, I have emerged unscathed.

I glance up at the hole I just fell through. It is several feet above me now. Even if I stand with my arms raised over my head, I won't be able to reach it. I could jump, grab on to the ledge, and pull myself back into it, but I am hoping there is another way out.

That small opening spills into a much larger room. The walls are jagged and glossy, the air musty and stagnant. There is an unsettling haze, a putrid odor from the stench of rotting flesh. I imagine the rogues have been feeding within these tunnels, and the overwhelming scent of decomposing meat makes me gag. I cover my mouth with my hand as bile rises in my chest. I taste the sharp, sour bite of vomit at the back of my throat and force it down.

Streams of dim light illuminate the space. It may not be sufficient for a human, but I can see well enough. Water pools at the edges of the room, with steady streams dripping down through cracks in the stone walls. The frost of winter has melted, making way for spring, and it has drenched the cave in its remains. The floors are sticky and slimy, and my boots slide against the rugged terrain.

I walk across the room, peering into the single tunnel that grants me an exit from this chamber. It is long and dark, and I walk the length of it, slowly, ever mindful that a rogue vampire may be moments away from catching me.

The tunnel is narrow, and the sides brush against my shoulders as I maneuver my way through. Like the other compartment, it seems to become smaller the longer I walk through it.

It opens to another room, this one much smaller than the last. And unlike the last pit, it opens to three more pathways.

I peer down each tunnel, seeing nothing that will help me decide which path to take. I worry where the wrong route will lead me. It already feels like I have been hiking this cave for hours. The occasional streams of light tell me it is past sunrise, and I am drowning in my anxiety over it.

I opt for the channel on the left, but after walking for several minutes, using my hands to navigate through the dark space, it stops at a dead end. I double back, telling myself wasting time like this is okay. I have to wait for sunset now anyway.

Next, I take the middle passage, and it mirrors the other one, but instead of stopping abruptly, it spills into a small room.

I notice the smell first. The rancid odor of rot is so potent it makes my eyes water. The air is thick, and I struggle to breathe without gagging. When I do vomit, I lurch forward, expelling the contents of an earlier blood bag onto the floor.

There is a step that leads me down into the room, but I don't take it. The rocky ground is covered in blood. The sight of it makes my innards cringe.

I am both astonished that rogues would waste this much food and regretful so many innocent lives were lost to a rogue nest we never knew existed. I made it my mission to protect the humans of Darkhaven, but I have failed spectacularly.

Inside the room, there are mounds of dead, decaying bodies. The air is tinged by something sweet, and I know this scent well. Death smells a lot like the acidic bite of overly ripened fruit, but unfortunately, it is masked by foulness. I think only someone with an excellent sense of smell could note the underlying aroma.

Still, even though I am blessed with heightened senses, I have to leave the room. I rush down the tunnel, nearly losing my footing when I emerge on the other side. I gulp down fresh air, ignoring the fact that it too smells like death—only to a lesser extent, but that is more than enough for me.

I glance at the final pathway, knowing that must be the one that will lead me to the rogues. I am both dreading taking it and optimistic that there will be more areas to explore. I am hopeful that I will be able to make it all day without seeing another vampire.

After taking a few minutes to collect myself, I venture down the final channel, nearly colliding with a sole rogue vampire. He seems surprised to see me, but as we make eye contact, he is quick to show his anger at my intrusion.

Growling low, snarling and baring fangs, he approaches

swiftly, slamming into me with a loud thump. The noise of my grunt, preceded by the even louder sound of us crashing to the ground, echoes through the chamber, and I am certain the other nearby rogues will overhear our quarrel. Still, I persist, not ready to give up just yet.

I hold him back with a hand pressed against his collarbone, and he snaps his jaw relentlessly, always only a few inches from making contact.

A rush of drool seeps from his jowls, splattering onto my cheeks. It drips down the curve of my jawline and seeps into my shirt. Again, I suppress the urge to vomit.

The rogue is small, similar in height and size to me, so I easily keep him at bay with just a single hand. With my free arm, I place the tips of my fingers at the narrowest part of his chest, right where the bone caves slightly, and I burrow deeply.

As I force my way through flesh, his eyes bulge from their sockets. His shock only strengthens my resolve.

I reach his heart quickly, and he bursts into ash, caking my skin where his spit moistened the area.

I jump to my feet, not wanting to be caught off guard by another rogue. I wait, gaze focused on the darkness ahead, but no one comes.

After several minutes pass, I allow myself to relax, believing our fight went unheard, so I ease up, rolling my shoulders to relieve the tension in my back. I wipe off his remains and continue forward.

The final tunnel looks like the others. The walls are sharp with jagged stone and slick from the melted snow that has seeped through cracks. I dodge streams of sunlight as I maneuver quietly around pools of water.

My mind is swirling, and my heart is racing, pounding

so loudly it is a wonder the other rogues haven't spotted me yet. I hate that I am on edge. My anxiety is making everything worse. I fear being caught before I am ready to make my presence known, and I worry about the dreamwalker. For all I know, his body is among the rotting heap one channel over. I have never felt so anxious before, especially in the midst of battle, when I am at my best.

I hear someone approaching. I flatten myself against the sticky wall and peer into the distance. The tunnel curves up ahead, so I still can't see him. But I hear him mumbling, complaining about his hunger and exhaustion.

There is nowhere to hide.

Quickly, I rush to where the tunnel curves, and I crouch beside the wall, trying my best to remain covered by the shadows. The rogue steps out from the darkness. He passes me and walks several paces before he stops abruptly.

Head cocked in the air, he inhales deeply, loudly. I listen as his lungs fill and expel the breath he took. He knows I am here. He smells me. He smells my fear.

I lunge forward, hoping to surprise him as I pounce. I land on his back, wrapping my legs around his torso. With one hand, I bury my fist into his hair, yanking his head backward. He peers at me, straining his eyes to fully see his attacker. He doesn't seem surprised to see me, but I haven't the time to ask why.

Guiding him by the scalp, I push his jaws away from my face. He growls as I do this, but I only hold on tighter. I only have seconds to subdue him before he pries me off.

From within my jacket, I withdraw the dagger Jasik gifted me after I became a vampire. Normally, I would fight another way, either by using my innate strength or by summoning the elements. But both are too risky during this encounter. Unlike the other rogue I killed earlier, this vampire is three times my size. I need to kill him before he kills me.

I thrust the blade into his chest, slicing through his heart. I hear the muscle shred as I make contact, and the rogue sucks in a deep, final breath.

When he erupts into ash, I fall to the ground. I spin around, holding out my dagger against possible assailants, but like before, no one comes. It is the early morning hours, which means it is a vampire's bedtime. Exhaustion weighs heavily on me, so I imagine the rogues are feeling it too.

I tiptoe down the tunnel until I reach another opening. This one is larger than the others combined. Like the others, it leads to even more pathways, and unfortunately, I will have to take each one individually.

The first three tunnels lead nowhere, either ending abruptly or spilling into a small room used for more . . . *storage*. I shudder when I think about the number of lives lost here. The smell of them decaying is getting easier to digest, but that realization nauseates me. It is a vicious cycle.

The fourth tunnel opens to another large room, but this one looks nothing like the others. It is vast, so expansive it is shocking to know I am still underground. The room is as wide as it is high, and the height of the room offers several platforms with tunnels that lead to other chambers within the cave system.

What is more worrisome is what this room contains. Several feet away, lying on the cold, wet, stone floor, there are dozens and dozens of rogue vampires—more in one place than I have ever seen before.

They have no idea I am here, and I must use this to my

advantage. It is only a matter of time before they wake, and like the other rogue I just killed, they will sense my fear. They will smell it, and they will find me.

I peer into the room, never fully setting a foot inside, and I search for the witch. Instead, I find more rogues, all asleep. There are too many for me to fight without using magic, so I know what I must do.

Preparing myself for one final merge, I grab the black onyx crystal and attempt to summon its magic, bringing forth the surge of darkness I used earlier tonight when I attacked my friends. Except this time, instead of being greeted by its power, it zaps me.

I hiss as it burns my flesh, yanking my hand free and shaking away the pain. Like before, it doesn't work, so I stare at it—just as unbelieving as I was earlier tonight. Blood pools in my hand, but slowly, my skin is healing. I gnaw on my lower lip, waiting for the pain to ease.

Something shifts in the room before me. The air changes subtly, and the shuffling sound of movement catches my full attention.

I look up, and I stare into the eyes of what is at least one hundred rogue vampires. Frozen in fear, I can't even scream. I can't breathe or move. All I can do is stare at them and hope this is all a really bad dream.

Almost in unison, they begin to close in. They lick their lips, eyes wide with excitement and hunger. I can practically taste their desire for me, and it makes my stomach churn.

Regaining my composure, I step backward, still cradling my hand as I contemplate my options. I can't run. There isn't anywhere I can hide that they won't find me. I can't seek refuge outside if the sun is up. And death certainly isn't a viable choice either.

For whatever reason, the amulet is choosing not to assist me, so I decide to rely on my own powers—something I should have done the moment I stepped into this godforsaken hell.

I summon the fire element quickly, using the heat of the stagnant air to fuel my calling, and balance the fireballs in both my hands. I think about the witch, and I consider yelling for him, urging him to join me. Together, we just may beat them.

But that plan is squashed, silenced by something far more sinister. While I was internally drafting my plan to encourage the dreamwalker to join forces with me, I was still moving backward, and now, I have collided with someone, the back of my body is now firmly against his.

He inhales deeply, breath fluttering my hair, and the sheer terror erupting within me is something I have never before experienced. I want to scream, but I suppress the desire. Instead, I spin around, readying myself to release a fireball, but I stop. My magic is smothered, flames extinguished.

My legs are weak, knees shaky. My arms tremble, my lip quivering. All at once, it feels like my heart is breaking, the pain like a thousand fingernails scratching away at my chest.

I wobble unsteadily, reaching for the walls of the cave to keep me upright. Even with the prickle at my skin alerting me to the dozens and dozens of gazes pinned at my back, the overriding anguish in who I am staring at is all I can feel.

"You can't be," I whisper.

I suck in a sharp breath, and my lip vibrates against my teeth, making a loud, squishy noise. My lungs ache from how fast my chest is heaving, and my eyes burn from the tears pouring down my cheeks. I don't bother stopping them. I let him see just how long I have mourned the loss of him.

"It's you," I say.

He smiles at me, his crimson eyes piercing the darkest of nights.

"*Hola, hija,*" he says, voice deep and smooth, just like I remember.

"*Papá.*"

ALSO BY DANIELLE ROSE

DARKHAVEN SAGA

Dark Secret

Dark Magic

Dark Promise

Dark Spell

Dark Curse

Dark Shadow

Dark Descent

Dark Power

Dark Reign

Dark Death

PIECES OF ME DUET

Lies We Keep

Truth We Bear

**For a full list of Danielle's other titles,
visit her at DRoseAuthor.com**

ACKNOWLEDGMENTS

Dark Descent takes Ava on her most difficult journey yet, one where she loses her moral compass to her darkest desires. This was both the hardest and most rewarding novel I have ever written. I hope you enjoy this next chapter as much as I do.

Publishing a book isn't easy, and I would not be where I am in my writing journey without help. I want to thank the countless people who have given Ava a chance—from booksellers and librarians who stock her story on their shelves, to readers who chat about the characters with friends, to my publishing team at Waterhouse Press who took a chance on an unknown author. Your support means more than I can ever describe.

ABOUT DANIELLE ROSE

Dubbed a "triple threat" by readers, Danielle Rose dabbles in many genres, including urban fantasy, suspense, and romance. The *USA Today* bestselling author holds a master of fine arts in creative writing from the University of Southern Maine.

Danielle is a self-professed sufferer of 'philes and an Oxford comma enthusiast. She prefers solitude to crowds, animals to people, four seasons to hellfire, nature to cities, and traveling as often as she breathes.

Visit her at DRoseAuthor.com

CONTINUE READING
THE DARKHAVEN SAGA

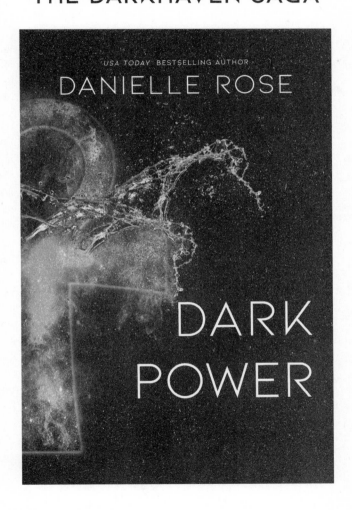